SUNDAYS *with* SULLIVAN

SUNDAYS *with*

SULLIVAN

HOW *THE ED SULLIVAN SHOW* BROUGHT ELVIS, THE BEATLES, AND CULTURE TO AMERICA

BERNIE ILSON

TAYLOR TRADE PUBLISHING
Lanham • New York • Boulder • Toronto • Plymouth, UK

Published by Taylor Trade Publishing
An imprint of The Rowman & Littlefield Publishing Group, Inc.
4501 Forbes Boulevard, Suite 200, Lanham, Maryland 20706
www.rlpgtrade.com

Estover Road, Plymouth PL6 7PY, United Kingdom

Distributed by NATIONAL BOOK NETWORK

Library of Congress Cataloging-in-Publication Data

Ilson, Bernie, 1924–
    Sundays with Sullivan : how the Ed Sullivan show brought Elvis, the Beatles, and culture to America / Bernie Ilson.
        p.   cm.
    Includes bibliographical references and index.
    ISBN-13: 978-1-58979-390-3 (cloth : alk. paper)
    ISBN-10: 1-58979-390-0 (cloth : alk. paper)
    ISBN-13: 978-1-58979-401-6 (electronic)
    ISBN-10: 1-58979-401-X (electronic)
    1. Ed Sullivan show (Television program).   2. Sullivan, Ed, 1901–1974.   I. Title.
PN1992.77.E35I47   2009
791.45'72—dc22   2008029915

♾ ™ The paper used in this publication meets the minimum requirements of American National Standard for Information Sciences—Permanence of Paper for Printed Library Materials, ANSI/NISO Z39.48-1992.

Manufactured in the United States of America.

*This book is dedicated with love and affection to my family:
my sons, David and Jimmy; their wives, Elyse and Rhonda;
my grandchildren, Emily and Sadie and Jesse and Sam;
and especially to my wonderful wife, the light of my life, Carol.*

Contents

Acknowledgments   ix

Introduction   xi

Part I: Behind the Scenes

1   An Unlikely Host   3

2   Ed Sullivan's Early Career   15

3   Working with Ed   25

4   A Complicated Man   33

5   The Columnist and His Competition   47

6   Elvis Presley, the Highest Paid Sullivan Guest   53

7   Ed Meets the Beatles   57

8   Mr. Sullivan Goes to Washington   71

9   When Ed Sullivan Broke Television's "Color Line"   77

10 Topo Gigio and the Obratsov Puppets   83

11 Sullivan Brings Opera and Classical Music to
    Television   89

12 Ed Speaks Out at the Fifteenth Anniversary of His
    Show   103

Part II: Insights and Observations

13 Marlo Lewis, First Producer of *The Ed Sullivan
    Show*, Reveals Its Growing Pains   115

14 Bob Precht, Producer of *The Ed Sullivan Show*,
    Comments on the Show and Its Cultural Aspects   119

15 Sol Hurok, an Impresario's Impression of *The Ed Sullivan Show* 129

16 A CBS Executive Offers Some Insights into the Success of *The Ed Sullivan Show* and Why It Was Cancelled 133

17 Larry Grossman, Former President of Public Broadcasting, Looks at the Cultural Impact of *The Ed Sullivan Show* 139

18 Paul Klein, Television Theorist, Discusses *The Ed Sullivan Show* and Television Viewing 145

19 Alvin Cooperman, Television and Broadway Producer, Takes an In-Depth Look at *The Ed Sullivan Show* 149

20 Artistic Directors and Managers of Opera and Dance Companies Reflect upon the Influence of *The Ed Sullivan Show* 155

21 The Critics Weigh In 161

22 Conclusion 173

Appendix A: *The Ed Sullivan Show* Ratings and Audience Share 181

Appendix B: Awards 183

Appendix C: *The Ed Sullivan Show* on DVD and VHS 185

Appendix D: Questionnaire and Cover Letter 189

Notes 193

Bibliography 201

Index 203

About the Author 215

Acknowledgments

I wish to acknowledge the great encouragement and help I have received from my family, associates, friends, and mentors in writing and researching this book. The project has taken more than a dozen years to complete, and it has been an enormously gratifying experience.

I offer my thanks to the artists, producers, television executives, theorists, and historians I interviewed for this book for giving me their time, information, and insight about their relationship to Ed Sullivan and *The Ed Sullivan Show*, as well as their valuable thoughts about popular culture, communications, and the arts. They are Bob and Betty Precht, Larry Grossman, Paul Klein, Alvin Cooperman, Bernard Gurtman, Jim Murtha, Robert Merrill, Irv Lichtman, Irwin Segelstein, Carmine Santullo, Marcie Levine, Tony Barrow, Paul McCartney, George Harrison, John Lennon, Ringo Starr, and Will Jordan, among others.

This book, in its early form, was the basis for my doctoral degree from New York University, and the help and encouragement I received from my committee and its professors was invaluable. I thank the late Dale McConathy for his initial support and Professors David Ecker, Judith Weissman, Marilynn Karp, and Terence Moran.

There are many friends and associates I wish to thank for their help and encouragement in writing and preparing this book for publication: Howard and Ken Mandelbaum at Photofest, Richard Friedman, Rob Precht, Ben Epstein, Kathy Epstein, Martin Hassner, Alan and Gail Baker, Donna and Al Malone, Marie-Jean and Martin Benis, Merilee and Herb Kaufman, Gil and Roz Gotfried, Marv and Naomi Duckler, Bob and Eleanor Schain, Myra and Zeff Ilson, and the kind people at the New York Public Library, especially at the Performing Arts Division, as well as those at the Museum of Television and Radio. I wish to thank Rick Rinehart, my editor at Taylor Trade Publishing, for visualizing a wider audience for this book and bringing it to his division at Rowman & Littlefield.

I want to especially acknowledge and thank Stephen Ryan of the Scarecrow Press for editing this book. It was Stephen who originally decided to take on the publishing of this book for Rowman & Littlefield. His advice, editorial judgment, and tireless effort helped to shape the book into its present form. Since this is my first book, I needed his experienced hand to guide me throughout the long editing process.

And, of course, I want to thank my family, who have always been my constant cheering section: David, Jimmy, Elyse, Rhonda, Emily, Sadie, Jesse, Sam, and most of all, Carol.

Introduction

Ed Sullivan invented a new way of presenting entertainment on television on his variety series titled, at first, *Toast of the Town*, which was also the name of his newspaper column about the celebrities in the world of show business and sports. It was a lively column filled with news, gossip, and gags about Broadway and Hollywood stars and would-be stars. The column appeared three times a week in the *New York Daily News*, at that time the number one newspaper (in terms of circulation) in America. Sullivan's column also ran in more than two hundred newspapers across the country. He was second in popularity to the King of Gossip Columnists, Walter Winchell.

Sullivan was forty-six when he first stepped onto the stage of the CBS Television Studio at the Empire Theater in New York City in 1948, as the host of his own hour-long variety show. No one expected this modest program would become television's longest running variety and music show, airing every Sunday night through 1971. Nor did anyone envision *The Ed Sullivan Show* bringing to television stars of the entertainment world such as Elvis Presley and the Beatles; Hollywood luminaries like Bing Crosby, Bob Hope, and Audrey Hepburn; some of Broadway's greatest actors and actresses including Helen Hayes and Fredric March; opera's most celebrated singers such as Maria Callas, Robert Merrill, and Joan Sutherland;

extraordinarily talented circus artists like Clyde Beatty and the high-wire walking Wallendas; unusual animal performers like Victor the Bear; and the world's foremost dance companies, including the Kirov, the Bolshoi, and the New York City Ballet.

The tone of this weekly one-hour program—always presented "live"—was set in the very first program, which featured Richard Rodgers and Oscar Hammerstein II, the leading Broadway musical composer and lyricist of that era; Jerry Lewis and Dean Martin, the top comedy team at that time; Kathryn Lee, a ballet dancer; Eugene List, a classical pianist; and John Kokoman, the winner of a local talent contest, who was New York City fireman. The elements of Sullivan's potpourri of entertainment—comedy, musical theater, ballet, classical music, and novelty performers—were evident in this very first program.

The lineup also represented another important Sullivan signature, one perhaps not as obvious. All of the performers, in some way, were "newsworthy," or to use the vernacular, "hot." They were personalities who were in the news, performers who were discussed in newspaper columns, magazines, or on the radio. Always the newspaperman, Sullivan was in tune with the public and their interest in seeing these hot personalities on television. Their taste was his taste.

But with an added twist.

Sullivan always strived to elevate the taste of his audience by inserting "drops of culture"—often only three or four minutes of "high-class" entertainment—into each show. He would present a scene from a Broadway show like *Camelot*, feature a classical violinist such as Isaac Stern, or spotlight a singer such as Roberta Peters, star of the Metropolitan Opera Company. It was not a coincidence that the singer who appeared on *The Ed Sullivan Show* the most times was Ms. Peters. She performed forty-one times on the program, much more than any popular singer. I do not believe that Sullivan planned his shows by thinking, "Let's add a little high culture to this week's lineup." Instead, he allowed his instincts to dictate dropping bits of culture gently into the mix of variety acts, and generally did so toward the end of each show.

Even after most other programs had switched to tape and film, Sullivan insisted that his variety show be presented live, feeling that it gave the program a spontaneity and edge that could not be achieved by taping it. Only occasionally—when the show originated from such far-flung locales as Spoleto, Italy; Moscow; or Munich—did Sullivan permit the show to be taped since, at that time, the facilities for telecasting the program live from overseas venues were not technically viable. However, the key element that made *The Ed Sullivan Show* different from its later imitators was that it reflected what was happening in the world of entertainment *at that moment* and presented it in a very professional manner. If Maria Callas appeared on the cover of *Time* magazine, chances were that Sullivan's booking team, or even Sullivan himself, was on the phone immediately to offer her a choice spot on next week's program.

Admittedly, Sullivan was not the most polished performer on television. In fact, his malapropisms and odd body and head movements were fodder for a horde of impressionists. Will Jordan, John Byner, David Frey, Rich Little, and a dozen other performers made a living by imitating and exaggerating Sullivan's voice patterns and stiff body movements. Was Ed upset with these impressionists? Of course not. Always the showman, Sullivan invited Will Jordan and the other imitators to appear on his show, and he laughed along with the audience. Sullivan understood that imitation is the highest form of flattery, and it helped to cement his reputation as a guy who could take a little ribbing.

Unlike other books about Ed Sullivan, this volume is written by someone who knew Ed Sullivan personally. I was the press representative for Sullivan Productions, the producers of *The Ed Sullivan Show* and Ed Sullivan television specials such as *The Beatles at Shea*

Stadium, *Clownaround*, and a dozen others that were carried nationally on CBS. The information and the anecdotes in this book are told firsthand from the point of view of an insider, not a person who needed to scour the libraries and old newspaper files. This book is an inside view of *The Ed Sullivan Show* and the unusual story of the most unlikely television star in the history of the medium.

SUNDAYS *with* SULLIVAN

Ed standing in the wings watching Gerry Marsden (of Gerry and the Pacemakers) perform. During the show, Ed's favorite place from which to watch the show was just offstage where he could rush back to center stage as needed. There was always a television monitor beside Ed so that he could see the program as it looked in the homes of millions of viewers. (Photofest)

1
An Unlikely Host

Ed Sullivan was the most powerful man in television.

And I was on the scene during many of his most exciting years as the press person for television's longest running variety series, *The Ed Sullivan Show*.

During the 1950s and 1960s, *The Ed Sullivan Show* was the premiere television showcase for talent in the world of entertainment, but, paradoxically, Ed Sullivan was not recognized for his unique and unusual ability to discover and present the new, most timely and exciting attractions in show business to a weekly audience of 35 million viewers.

Sullivan brought the Beatles, the Bolshoi Ballet, Maria Callas, Elvis Presley, and hundreds of Hollywood's major film stars—Bob Hope, Walt Disney, Fred Astaire, Bing Crosby, Julie Andrews, Ingrid Bergman, and Gary Cooper—to television, many for their first appearance on the medium, but his detractors, and there were many, did not acknowledge his ability to reach grassroots America and entertain them.

The press pilloried Sullivan, the man who reinvented variety entertainment for television even though he was a nationally syndicated columnist for his entire working life. Perhaps, filled with envy, his critics decried the fact that one of their own had vaulted to the top of a new medium. The press, especially the television critics and columnists, chided him for his stumbling speech patterns, frequent malapropisms, and obvious unease on stage, missing the point that

Bing Crosby made his television debut on *The Ed Sullivan Show* in 1950. He is pictured here with Sullivan on stage during the interview section of the program. (Photofest)

Sullivan was always the final word on who would appear on his show. He was the behind-the-scenes force from the very beginning in 1948 and had been instrumental in booking the show (especially during the first ten years of the series), setting the lineup of the acts and the pace of the show so that it presented the newest, most talented performers in films, theater, opera, and dance. Instead of trying to hide his lack of stage presence, Sullivan gloried in it and invited impersonators to build comedy routines around his seeming ineptness as a performer. Will Jordan, John Byner, Norm Crosby, and a half a dozen other comedians performed repeatedly on *The Ed Sullivan Show* and caricatured the antics of its host. Surprisingly, the person who laughed loudest was Sullivan himself.

I think that Will Jordan's impression of Ed Sullivan, the stiff walk, the bulging eyes, the stumbling speech, was copied and expanded upon by others until the caricature eventually became the vision that the public accepted as the "real Ed Sullivan." When I recently viewed dozens of early shows, I realized how outlandish the impressionists were and how far they went to get a laugh. This seemed to be all right with Sullivan, who was smart enough to book impressionists like Will Jordan and Rich Little to perform their exaggerated takeoffs of his speech and movement mannerisms to build the Sullivan image as a "nice guy" in the minds of the public.

So what was the secret of Sullivan's enormous success, a show that was one of television's top-rated programs for a record twenty-three years? I believe that part of the secret was the creative and extraordinarily competent team he assembled to produce a weekly show with new sets, new costumes, new dance numbers and musical arrangements each week. This kind of preparation for a weekly television show is unheard of in today's television schedule. In addition, *The Ed Sullivan Show* was a "live" program. During the entire run of the series, beginning on June 20, 1948, at 8:00 p.m. on Sunday night, *The Ed Sullivan Show* was presented "live from New York City" over the CBS Television Network, at first from the stage of Maxine Elliott Theater on West 39th Street and Broadway, and later from CBS Studio 50 at 52nd Street and Broadway, which was renamed the Ed Sullivan Theater in 1967. (The only live weekly entertainment series on television today is *Saturday Night Live* on NBC, which is not a prime-time show.)

To contrast *The Ed Sullivan Show* with today's television, when the NBC series *ER* decided to televise the premiere program of its 1998 season as a live show, there was a mountain of publicity about how unusual and unique this was. Just imagine, NBC Television considered that telecasting *ER* live was an important event, in fact, a unique event. And more recently when NBC presented the first episode of the final season of *Will and Grace* as a live show, again the television columnists hailed it as a special event. No one seemed to remember that *The Ed Sullivan Show* did more than one thousand live programs, continuing the live format long after most of its competition had gone to film and tape shows. (Perhaps, many of today's television columnists were just tots when the Sullivan shows were originally aired or were born after 1971, when the show went off the air.)

The Ed Sullivan Show was not telecast live for its publicity value. Sullivan insisted that the program be *live*. He knew that the performers would be on their toes if they were aware there would be no retakes. *Live* meant adrenaline, spontaneity, excitement, as well as a few mistakes and bloopers. There was also an audience of 720 people at the rehearsal show at 1:00 p.m. in the afternoon, as well as the actual telecast at 8:00 p.m.

Ed Sullivan believed that the rehearsal show audience would react to the comedians, singers, dancers, acrobats, and rock groups the same way the television audience across the country would when the show was telecast later in the day at 8:00 p.m. Sullivan did not call it a survey or a test audience, but that was exactly what they were. After each rehearsal show, Sullivan and his producer— Marlo Lewis during the early years, and Bob Precht for the last thirteen years—would make adjustments based on how well the acts went over with the rehearsal audience.

When Ed Sullivan was admitted to the Television Hall of Fame, he was no longer alive but on his cozy cloud up there somewhere. Ed must be laughing, because he had the last laugh on all the critics who tore into him each week as he steered the *The Ed Sullivan Show* to a record twenty-three years of entertaining the 35 million people each week who eagerly watched the most popular variety show ever to grace the tinseled tube.

Was he that good? It depends on your definition of "good." Sullivan was unique. Ed was probably the most improbable person to emcee a major variety show outside of Joe Franklin. In reviewing his qualifications, one must admit that he had a rumbling way of walking to the middle of the stage, and when he got there, he seemed to forget what he was going to say. He often mispronounced the name of the guest star, and once actually said, "Let's have a hand for 'Ave Maria.'" He read his introductions off a teleprompter only six feet in front of him, and stumbled over the words, even though Ed had written the script himself.

So why do many critics of today now call the show "the best variety program ever on television"? Why do repeats of the program, packaged as "The Best of Sullivan" television specials, garner great reviews and large viewing audiences. It's obvious that to those who watched the show or the repeats, *The Ed Sullivan Show* was entertaining, timely, and presented the most popular performers of the day. It was a combination *of The Tonight Show with Jay Leno, The Late Show with David Letterman, The Today Show*, the Arts and Entertainment Channel, Public Television, MTV, the Nashville Network, and a dozen other TV channels rolled into one big, fast-moving package that burst onto the TV screen all over America each Sunday night at 8:00 p.m.

I believe that Sullivan's place in the history of television is secure because Sullivan invented the form and developed it into what we call a television variety show. But in reality, it was much more than that. Certainly it had vaudeville acts, but it also had all sorts of celebrities and people in the news. For example, when the Mets won the World Series in 1969, Ed had the whole team on stage the very next day. When Arcaro won the Kentucky Derby, Ed had him take a bow from the audience and gave him a healthy honorarium. When Gian Carlo Menotti created the Spoleto Festival, Ed took his show to Spoleto, Italy, and added Louis Armstrong to Menotti's opera singers and a scene from a Tennessee Williams play. Sullivan did a series of shows early on from the stage of the Metropolitan Opera but soon discovered that the Sullivan audience could only take three minutes of opera, and from then on it was high culture presented in small drops. But culture was there in almost every show.

To understand why CBS selected Ed Sullivan to be the host of their first prime-time variety series, you must imagine who Ed Sullivan was in 1948, the year the program first aired on television. Ed Sullivan was a forty-six-year-old, handsome, athletic, square-shouldered man, who had been a newspaper columnist all of his adult life.

Three times a week, Sullivan's column appeared in the *New York Daily News*, a paper a million New Yorkers read each morning. It was also the newspaper with the largest circulation in America. Sullivan's column, "Toast of the Town," also appeared in two hundred newspapers all over America via the *Chicago Tribune* Syndicate; however, Sullivan was not the King of Gossip Columnists. That title belonged to Walter Winchell, whose column for the rival *New York Daily Mirror* and the Hearst Newspaper syndicate and who often "scooped" the others with information supplied by his assistants and by legions of unpaid press agents seeking to get their clients' names and activities into his very influential column that was read and discussed by everyone: housewives and their friends, office workers and their colleagues during their coffee breaks, and subway travelers on their way to work. It was the water cooler column of its day.

From the 1930s, '40s, and through the beginning of the '50s was the heyday of the gossip columnists. Winchell, Sullivan, Earl Wilson, Leonard Lyons, Louis Sobel, Dorothy Kilgallen, and Bob Sylvester in New York and Louella Parsons, Hedda Hopper, Sidney Skolsky, and Jimmy Fiddler in Los Angeles were eagerly read by an interested public all over America. Newspapers across the country ran syndicated versions of the columns of these celebrated columnists, who wrote about new movies and plays, divorces and "blessed events," scandals and secrets of celebrities, politicians and socialites in the columnist's often picturesque prose.

The columnists had power. A line in Winchell's column about a new movie starlet could send her career rocketing ahead. A twenty-word review praising a new Broadway show could produce lines of ticket buyers at the box office the next day, and conversely, a bad notice about a nightclub revue might mean disaster for the club. Winchell was known for awarding "orchids" for a good performance, but his occasionally cutting remarks could dent a career or even lead to the closing of a show.

Ed Sullivan was a close second to Winchell in his "clout," but Sullivan seldom used his power to knock a performance. If Sullivan did not like a performance, he usually just avoided writing about it. His column was lighter, newsier, and sometimes almost sentimental. He wrote mostly about entertainers, and he loved to mingle with famous and talented sports figures. An excellent golfer, Sullivan was friends with the stars of the sporting world. Sullivan started his newspaper career as a sports columnist and only later turned to covering Hollywood and Broadway.

His sporting pals included former heavyweight Jack Dempsey, boxer Johnny Dundee, and golfer Gene Sarazen. It was not by chance that Sullivan featured appearances of stars of the sports world on *The Ed Sullivan Show*. He liked and admired these champion sportsmen.

Bob Precht, the producer of *The Ed Sullivan Show* for the last thirteen years it was on the air, explained how Sullivan used his newspaper training and instincts to find talent for the show:

Ed Sullivan was constantly out on the town seeking material for his syndicated newspaper column, and he would be aware of what was

Ed looks obviously delighted with a comedy exchange with boxing champion Rocky Marciano. (Photofest)

happening in the entertainment world. For instance, if a sensational new opera star suddenly appeared on the scene, Ed would be there to catch the performance. Similarly, if a new Broadway show premiered, Ed would see it, because he was on the First Night press list. He was very aware of everything happening in the [show] business such as a new chanteuse at the Blue Angel or a break-through new comic at the Copacabana. A great part of Ed's success was that he had a "catholic" interest in the whole world of entertainment, which went from vaudeville to nightclubs to the classical concert stage. He covered them all.[1]

Precht continued comparing the programming of the Sullivan Show to the lineup of acts on a vaudeville bill: "Ed understood that in vaudeville, you started slow and built to the star's turn, which was the next-to-closing act. That went out the window with television, because you had to grab the audience and hold them for an hour. Sullivan would open with the big act, and then bring that headliner back later in the show for a second or third turn. Ed knew you had to capture the audience right at the top of the show, and keep them entertained for 60 minutes."[2]

When the Beatles first appeared on *The Ed Sullivan Show* on February 9, 1964, they opened the show, and later Ed brought them back in the second half for two more spots. In fact, every time the Beatles played the Sullivan show—a total of ten appearances—they always opened the show.

When *The Ed Sullivan Show* neared its twentieth anniversary, the press—which had been indifferent, condescending, but seldom laudatory toward the show—began to realize that the longevity and success of the program was in large part due to the talent of Sullivan as a programmer and discoverer of newsworthy talent. *Time* magazine and *Life* magazine both did features on Sullivan at that time. In the *Time* issue of October 13, 1967, their television editor wrote, "In the quick-shift sudden death world of television, only two things are constant: commercials and Ed Sullivan."[3]

Feeling that the twentieth anniversary was a real television milestone, the *Time* editor continued,

> While the rest of the [television] industry celebrates a three year run as something akin to a three minute mile, Sullivan is hosting his 20th season on the longest running show in the history of TV. Governments have fallen, wars have been won and lost, generations have passed into manhood, but the Mount Rushmore of TV endures. Each season the reappearance of his granite visage on Sunday evening inevitably provokes the same question, What exactly is Ed Sullivan's talent?
>
> He doesn't sing. He doesn't dance.

He doesn't tell jokes—at least not intentionally. His malapropisms ("I would like to prevent a new singer"), his carny-barker pleas for applause ("Let's hear it for the Lord's Prayer"), and his penchant for forgetting names (Singer Polly Bergen is invariably introduced as Barbara Britton), are part of TV lore.[4]

The *Time* editor moved close to the truth when he wrote of Sullivan,

As the single most influential star maker in TV, he shrewdly uses his power to gather, pay for, juggle, condense, cut or otherwise shape the talent to the needs of the show. He takes no guff from stars, advertisers or agents. When Beatles manager Brian Epstein told him, "I would like to know the exact wording of your introduction," Sullivan coldly replied, "I would like you to get lost." The one influence that guises his taste is "public opinion, which is the voice of God." The voice—as revealed to Sullivan—speaks on Sunday afternoons, when an audience is invited to watch the dress rehearsal. Pacing the stage like a disgruntled midwife, Sullivan keeps his baleful blue eyes on the hall. What the audience likes he likes, and performers have come to recognize a certain pursing of the lips as the kiss of death. After the run-through, he huddles with his son-in-law, Producer Bob Precht, and jiggers the sequence of acts, deletes some, and pares others from 10 minutes to 90 seconds.[5]

The editor from *Time* discovered that Ed Sullivan had his own idea of what a television host should be. Sullivan explained, "There's too much damn talk on TV. . . . Other variety shows have skillful and amusing hosts, but they spend too much time getting into the act. The most difficult thing in the world is to shut up. Besides, whoever said that a master of ceremonies had to be a glamour boy? What counts is the kind of product he puts out."[6]

The article closed with the question about Sullivan still not completely answered for the editor from *Time* as he concluded, "Now 65, Sullivan is mumbling again about retiring, but no one believes him. Sure as Mass on Sunday, Old Stone Face will be back next season with yet another 'reely big shew' and everyone will be asking the old question. Perhaps the best answer is given by an old Sullivan regular, comic Alan King, 'Ed does nothing,' he says, 'But he does it better than anyone else on television.'"[7]

A week later in *Life*, the most popular magazine of the 1960s, Wayne Warga wrote another kind of a piece about the twentieth anniversary of *The Ed Sullivan Show*. *Life*, a "picture magazine," ran a series of photographs of Sullivan and performers who appeared on his show. Warga followed Sullivan around for a week or so and the text of the article took a more personal slant than the one in *Time*. Warga was at the rehearsal show and witnessed Sullivan at work. He described Sullivan's Sunday routine, detailing each minute reaction from the television host: from the afternoon rehearsal, through the actual program as each performer was introduced, and after the show's conclusion, when Sullivan would confer with Bob Precht in an hour or so editing session. Warga remarked with wonder the seemingly scant amount of time Sullivan spent on each week's show—in Warga's estimation a mere two hundred minutes—and was impressed how it all came together under one man's supervision.[8]

Ed Sullivan's Early Career

To understand the nature of *The Ed Sullivan Show*, it is important to understand the persona of the host of the series. Edward Vincent Sullivan was born in New York City on September 28, 1901, one of a set of twins. His brother Daniel was a sickly infant and passed away at the age of nine months. When young Ed was four, the family decided that living on 114th Street in Harlem was not good for the children and moved to Port Chester, New York, a small rural town near the Connecticut border. It was there where Ed Sullivan grew up, went to school, and excelled in athletics. He was already interested in journalism and in high school covered sports for the local newspaper, the *Port Chester Item*. He was paid one dollar a column, quite a good amount for a high school student learning the trade of writing. Sullivan did so well that when he graduated from high school, the *Item* offered him a regular job as a reporter at the salary of twelve dollars a week. Among his assignments were writing obituaries and covering the police court scene, but it was sports that interested him most. One of Sullivan's big moments as a reporter for the *Item* occurred when baseball player Babe Ruth came through Port Chester to play an exhibition game. Sullivan interviewed him and, for a while, became a local celebrity because of his closeness to the great ballplayer.

When he was twenty-one, Sullivan was drawn away from the *Port Chester Item* by the sports editor of the *New York Evening Mail* to cover high school sports. It was an opportunity for Sullivan to move into the New York newspaper scene, and he made the most of it. In less than a year, he was moved up to covering golf, tennis, and college sports. Sullivan learned the game of golf as a teenager when he was a caddy at the Westchester Country Club and developed into an excellent golfer; he continued to play the game most of his life. Another young caddy at the club was Gene Sarazen, who went on to become one of the greatest professional golfers in the game, winning the Masters and the Open. Sullivan and Sarazen were friendly as youngsters, and the friendship continued as Sullivan went up the ladder as a journalist and Sarazen continued his climb to the peak of the golf world. Over the years, Sullivan made many strong friendships with famous athletes such as boxing champions Jack Dempsey and Joe Louis, and dozens of baseball and football players.

At the *Mail*, Sullivan's salary was seventy-five dollars a week, a goodly sum for a single young man at that time. It enabled him to upgrade his lifestyle. He bought an automobile and started to wear custom-made suits. Sullivan always believed in dressing well, and his success in journalism and his later success in television were signaled by attention to sartorial matters.

It was during his tenure at the *Mail* that Sullivan began to frequent nightclubs and the theater. He took an apartment on West 48th Street, in the center of the theatrical district near his favorite nightclub, the Silver Slipper. He was frequently at the club, where he made friends with many performers including the comedy team of Clayton, Jackson, and Durante. Sullivan often played golf with Lou Clayton and Jimmy Durante, who later went on to solo fame. Durante became a lifelong friend.

All these friendships helped Sullivan when he later became a Broadway columnist and still later with *The Ed Sullivan Show*.

Just as Sullivan thought he was on his way to success as a sports writer, the *Mail* was sold to the *Sun*, another daily New York newspaper, and the *Sun* discontinued publishing the *Mail*. Temporarily out of work, Sullivan accepted writing positions with a series of newspapers. *The Philadelphia Ledger* offered him a job, and he moved briefly to that city before returning to New York City to work for the *New York Bulletin*. Other short-term jobs followed at the *Leader* and finally the *Morning Telegraph*, where he remained for two years until 1927. At that time, Bernarr MacFadden, an eccentric health enthusiast who made a fortune publishing sensational magazines such as *True Stories*, published the *Graphic*, a New York tabloid. MacFadden's decision to publish a daily New York paper shook up the New York newspaper world.

MacFadden started the *Graphic* in 1924, and in 1927 he decided to add a Saturday sports section. Sullivan was hired to work as a reporter for the new section, and it turned out to be one of the most important moves of his journalistic career.

MacFadden was an eccentric in the true sense. He often walked twenty miles to his Manhattan office from his home in Westchester. He was usually barefoot, and he was a strict vegetarian. Also, MacFadden often dressed in Roman-type robes and wore his hair long, to his shoulders. Even Sullivan considered him a little weird, but he always called him "Mr. MacFadden."

The *Graphic* had a coterie of gossip columnists, the most famous of whom was Walter Winchell. Louis Sobol wrote a Broadway column and was also one of the "stars" of the paper. They were a little older than Sullivan, who was twenty-six at the time, but Sullivan took to calling everyone "kid" or "kiddo," a habit he continued throughout his life.

The *Graphic* began sinking under a sea of red ink by 1930, and the popular columnists began to jump ship. Walter Winchell left for a job at the *New York Mirror*, and Louis Sobol made plans to leave the paper, too. It was then that MacFadden asked Ed Sullivan to move from the sports department to the entertainment desk and to write a Broadway column. Sullivan did this reluctantly because he truly liked sports reporting, but it proved to be another turning point in his career.

Sullivan had been secretly upset at the gossip columnist, personified by Walter Winchell, who doted on revealing upcoming divorces and scandals. So Sullivan, who had always been a straight-laced person on morals and marriage, surprised everybody with his first column by berating the columnists for their approach.

In his opening column in the *Graphic* on June 1, 1931, Sullivan wrote,

> I charge the Broadway columnists with defaming the street [Broadway]. I entered a field of writing that ranks so low that it is difficult to distinguish one columnist from his road companions. I have entered a field, which offers scant competition. The Broadway columnists have lifted themselves to distinction by borrowed gags, gossip that is not always kindly, and keyholes that often reveal what might be better hidden. . . . In my capacity as a drama critic, I pledge you of the theater that if I like a show I will say so, without ambiguities of phrasing that might protect my *Variety* box score.[1] With the theater in the doldrums, it means a decisive voice, and I promise to supply it.[2]

The other Broadway columnists were incensed by Sullivan's assertions and reacted with columns calling Sullivan to task, but others lauded him for his stand. Although Sullivan's column did deal in gossip, it was always with a light hand and with the knowledge that he did not want to hurt a person's reputation. In the 1930s and '40s, Sullivan attained prominence as a nationally syndicated columnist after he joined the *New York Daily News* just before the demise of the *Graphic* in 1932. Sullivan was overshadowed by Walter Winchell, who controlled the number one spot in the Broadway column field for decades.

Sullivan's reference to the Broadway theater scene in his very first column reinforces the proposition that Sullivan was a lifelong devotee of the theater. He once said that Helen Hayes, often called "the first lady of the theater," was his favorite guest on his television show. He respected and admired fine acting, and it is no accident that when he put on a scene from James Agee's Broadway drama *All the Way Home*, the show, which had been scheduled to close, received a spurt of theatergoers during the next weeks. The show went on to win the Pulitzer Prize and have a year run on the Great White Way. The producer, Arthur Cantor, has said that the appearance of a scene from *All the Way Home* on the Sullivan show saved the production from closing prematurely.

A week before the *Graphic* closed its doors on July 7, 1932, Joseph Patterson, president of the *New York Daily News*, called Ed Sullivan and offered him a job as a columnist. The salary was only two hundred dollars a week, less than he had been earning at the *Graphic*, but Sullivan wisely accepted the position. His column, "Toast of the Town," was later syndicated nationally by the *Chicago Tribune/New York Daily News* Syndicate to more than two hundred newspapers. Sullivan remained with the *Daily News*, writing his column continuously until his death. With his overriding fame as a television producer and master of ceremonies, few viewers outside of New York City, where the *Daily News* was the most popular newspaper, realized that Ed Sullivan wrote a Broadway column three times a week during the twenty-three-year-run of his show. For Sullivan it was a labor of love, and he always considered himself as "first a newspaperman, and second a television host and producer."

In the 1930s and early 1940s, radio flourished. Millions of radios were sold, and a new breed of radio stars burst onto the national scene. Jack Benny, Eddie Cantor, *Fibber MaGee and Molly*, Fred Allen, and Burns and Allen were a few of the popular performers on this new medium. Their shows were eagerly awaited by the entire family, who gathered in front of the new radios to listen to their jokes and songs. Radio also presented the Broadway and gossip columnists with an opportunity to reach their ever-growing public. It was at this time that Walter Winchell hit the peak of his popularity with his weekly Sunday radio show, which was broadened to include "inside news" about political figures as well as gossip about Hollywood and Broadway celebrities. Sullivan also had a radio show on which he interviewed actors, actresses, and sports figures in the limelight. Winchell drew the biggest audiences with his "scoops" about the famous and infamous of the day, and Sullivan played "second fiddle" until television moved into the forefront of media in the late '40s.

As part of his work for the *New York Daily News*, Sullivan served as master of ceremonies for the newspaper's yearly Harvest Moon Ballroom competition, in which amateur dancers competed for prizes and recognition as the "best waltz team" or the "best tango team" and other categories. The finals of the competition were held at Madison Square Garden. One of the prizes of the competition was a week's appearance at the Loew's State Theater, a Broadway vaudeville venue. As master of ceremonies, Sullivan was to introduce the six dance teams at the State Theater stage show. It was not a complicated chore. Sullivan was not expected to tell jokes or entertain the audience. He was there just to introduce the dance teams. In addition to the appearances in vaudeville, during World War II, the Harvest Moon winners accompanied Sullivan to Army and Navy installations near New York City to entertain the servicemen. Both assignments prepared Sullivan for his later calling in life.

Sullivan and his wife, Sylvia, were the ultimate show business couple. Their whole life revolved around Sullivan's work as a Broadway columnist and entertainment critic for his syndicated column. The daily column appeared in newspapers nationwide during

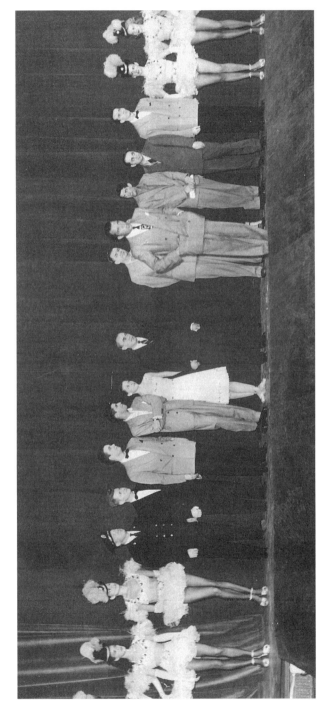

Ed Sullivan and the cast of the first Ed Sullivan show (June 20, 1948), then called *Toast of the Town*. *Left to right:* Two Toastette dancers, singing New York City fireman John Kokoman, classical pianist Eugene List, comedian Lee Goodman (of the team of Kirkwood and Goodman), comedian Jerry Lewis (of the team of Martin and Lewis), ballerina Kathryn Lee, composer Richard Rodgers, lyricist Oscar Hammerstein, Ed Sullivan, singer-comedian Dean Martin, boxing referee Ruby Goldstein, comedian Jimmy Kirkwood, and two Toastette dancers. (Photofest)

the 1940s, 1950s, and l960s, syndicated by the powerful *New York Daily News/Chicago Tribune* Syndicate. The Sullivans lived at the Delmonico Hotel on Park Avenue and East 59th Street where they had a large three-bedroom suite. There were two entrances to their apartment, which was on the eleventh floor. The door to 1102 led to Ed Sullivan's large one-room office, which originally had been a bedroom. Sullivan and his assistant, Carmine Santullo, worked there on the column each morning. The 1101 entrance opened into the full apartment. There was a foyer that opened into a large living room, which was very tastefully decorated with several comfortable looking French-style couches and Morris chairs. Vases of fresh flowers in large ceramic vases were everywhere. The walls of the living room were covered, almost to the ceiling, with dozens of paintings and drawings. There was one Monet and a large Don Kingman watercolor as well as a small oil by Xavier Cugat, a popular Latin bandleader.

There was no full-size kitchen in the apartment, just a small one almost the size of a closet, which was used for snacks and coffee. Ed and Sylvia took almost all of their meals at nearby restaurants and always went out for dinner to one of their favorite eating spots, such as Gino's on Lexington Avenue. They rarely stayed home at night. Ed and Sylvia were usually "out on the town" attending the opening of a Broadway show or catching the performance of the latest new singer or comedian at one of New York's many nightclubs. It was also his business to view the nightclub and theater performances so that he could comment about them in his column. At the night spots and theaters, Sullivan would gather information and tidbits of news for "Toast of the Town." As with all of the columnists, Sullivan had his large group of friendly managers and press agents who would "feed him" information about the Broadway and Hollywood scene.

Over the years, Sullivan became friendly with scores of stars,

Ed Sullivan in his office at the Delmonico Hotel, at Park Avenue and East 59th Street in New York City. His office and apartment were adjacent on the eleventh floor of the Delmonico. (Photofest)

their agents, and their press representatives, and in a large sense, these contacts and friendships helped the Columbia Broadcasting System executives select him as the host of a new television variety series they planned to telecast beginning in June 1948. It was actually Worthington Miner, an important executive producer at CBS and a friend of Sullivan's, who approached the columnist with the offer to host his own variety show. Sullivan quickly accepted.

Working with Ed

I had close involvement with *The Ed Sullivan Show* as its director of publicity from 1963 through the end of the series in 1971, and in this role I set up scores of media interviews and appearances for Sullivan. I also attended all of the Sunday performances and dress rehearsals and had an opportunity to be an "insider" at Sullivan productions. My first contact with the program, however, took place several years earlier.

While I was still in college, I began to work in the publicity department of the Shubert Theater Productions, and later for a series of Broadway press agents who "fed" gossip and news about their clients to newspaper columnists such as Walter Winchell, Dorothy Kilgallen, Leonard Lyons, and, of course, Ed Sullivan.[1] I would contact Sullivan, or his assistant, Carmine Santullo, and submit news items and anecdotes about our clients for inclusion in his column. At that time, the Broadway column was an important venue for bringing our clients, especially our show business clients, to the attention of Broadway and Hollywood producers and the public in general. Since these columns appeared not only in New York City newspapers but in hundreds of newspapers all over America via the news services and syndicates, the column items could bring fame and fortune to our clients. I studied the format of all of the columns including Sullivan's, which appeared in the *New York Daily News* and hundreds of other newspapers nationwide through the *New York Daily News/Chicago Tribune* Syndicate. Sullivan liked short, snappy items, seldom more than two or three lines, about the lives and work of celebrities. He also ran one-line jokes (attributed to our clients, but written by the press agent) usually of a topical nature.

For a short while I left the ranks of press agents to become a manager of variety acts. I represented comedians, dancers, and singers. During those years, in the early and middle 1950s, I arranged for many of my clients to appear on *The Ed Sullivan Show*. Most of the time I contacted one of the bookers of the show, such as Jack Babb or Mark Leddy, but occasionally, when it was an important act that required "serious money," I would contact Sullivan directly. One of those acts was a dance troupe called the Ballet Españoles.

I knew the manager of the group, David Libidins, who had brought the troupe to America for a ten-city tour. I contacted Sullivan and suggested that he book the group on his show just prior to their American tour, and Sullivan bought it. I had Libidins bring the Ballet Españoles to New York a few days before the tour, and they appeared on the show performing one of their flamenco numbers. They were a success, and it opened the door for me to present other attractions of this kind to Sullivan. For a short while, I was Sullivan's Spanish connection. This relationship ended when I left the management field to accept a job with NBC Television as a writer in their fledgling Comedy Development project.

A few years later, I returned to the publicity field and joined Rogers and Cowan, the foremost PR (public relations) agency in the entertainment field. I quickly rose to head of their television department in New York. *The Ed Sullivan Show* was one of Roger and Cowan's clients, and so I renewed my relationship with Sullivan and his producer, Bob Precht. I would often "cover" the show and became a frequent visitor backstage. A few years later, Sullivan discovered that Rogers and Cowan were also representing shows on

ABC Television and NBC Television that were in the same time slot as the Sullivan show, Sunday night at 8:00 p.m. Feeling that this was a great conflict of interest, Sullivan fired Rogers and Cowan.

A few weeks later, I received a call from Bob Precht, and he suggested I meet him and Sullivan. Their intent was obvious. Sullivan and Precht wanted me to leave Rogers and Cowan and work for Sullivan Productions. I informed Henry Rogers of my conversation with Bob Precht, and he said that I should meet with Sullivan. At the meeting, Precht and Sullivan suggested that I join their company as the "inside" PR representative. I countered by saying that I would love to work for them but would prefer to open my own PR agency with the Sullivan show as my first client. Sullivan and Precht accepted my suggestion, and I returned to Rogers and Cowan and told Henry Rogers about the offer. Henry, who had been my mentor at the agency, realized that it was a unique opportunity for me and told me to accept the offer. He also added, "If it doesn't work out, you could always come back and work for me." Rogers remained a good friend and even sent me clients (who might have conflicted with other clients he had on his roster or could not pay Roger and Cowan's high fees).

The CBS Press Department took care of the routine publicity chores of sending out news releases and informational sheets listing the performers for each week's show, as well as supplying newspaper and magazine editors with photographs of the performers. It was my job to set up the strategy of presenting *The Ed Sullivan Show* as the premier variety series on television. As part of this strategy, I selected the most outstanding upcoming performers that were booked to appear on the show and arranged interviews between them and television editors of major newspapers and wire services. Each article appeared just prior to the performer's appearance on the Sullivan show and was valuable in promoting the

Left to right: Ed Sullivan; Bernie Ilson, director of public relations for Ed Sullivan Productions; and media consultant Tom Quirk at a Sullivan Production media party in the 1960s. (Photofest)

guest's appearance. It was also critical to building an audience for the Ed Sullivan television series, one of the key aspects of the PR campaign.

I also set up appearances for Ed Sullivan on television and radio programs to promote special shows, as well as scores of interviews with magazines such as *TV Guide*, *Life* magazine, and the *New York Times*. Probably the most important part of my PR work was acting as a spokesperson for the show with the media. Over the years, Sullivan had several public arguments with hosts of other television shows, such as Jack Paar and Steve Allen, and with disgruntled performers like Jackie Mason. The CBS Press Department declined to be involved in anything that hinted at controversy, so I became the spokesperson for Sullivan Productions in these matters.

Above all, Ed Sullivan was a professional newspaperman. He always thought of his show as if he were writing a column. The show had to be topical, exciting, and start off with a great "lead." But he also had an unusual instinct for finding a performer who had that special "magic" to become a great star. I have had a good deal of experience in dealing with very successful people. I believe that for anyone to rise to the top of their profession, they must be smart, persistent, ingenious, opportunistic, and willing to work a sixteen-hour day. Sullivan had all of those qualities. Although he was somewhat star-struck (he enjoyed being in the company of celebrities such as Fred Astaire, Bing Crosby, Robert Merrill, and Maria Callas), his personal friends—those he and Sylvia would go to dinner with—were not often the major stars. For instance, he often dined with singer Jerry Vale and his wife, Rita, not a big star, but a friend. He enjoyed the company of sports personalities like Jack Dempsey, but very often he would have dined just with his family: his wife, Sylvia; their daughter, Betty Precht; and her husband, Bob Precht, the producer of the Sullivan show.

Sullivan never had an entourage or a band of cronies. He would often take walks down Park Avenue or stroll through Central Park alone or with a friend. Sometimes, I would walk him home from the television studio to his apartment at the Delmonico on Park Avenue and East 59th Street. He would often be stopped by passersby who recognized him. When strangers asked for an autograph, Sullivan was always happy to comply with their requests, often asking the person's name so he could personalize it. I never saw him refuse to give a fan an autograph. He was also very loyal to those who worked for him. He rarely fired people, and many remained with the show for its entire run, including orchestra leader Ray Block, booker Mark Leddy, and his assistant, Carmine Santullo, who was his right-hand man for forty years.

Sullivan had a reputation for having a strong temper, but I only saw him very upset one time, and that was at Jackie Mason, who he felt made an obscene gesture to the audience on his show. Sullivan's

Ed Sullivan and his wife, Sylvia, with their daughter, Betty, in their apartment at the Delmonico Hotel in the early 1950s. (Photofest)

backstage outburst at Mason made the front pages in the New York newspapers, only because Mason went directly to the press to complain about being "fired."

Ed had a knack for personally letting a star or a friend know that he appreciated his or her work or talent or contribution to the Sullivan show. He would spend hours writing personal notes to the stars who appeared on his show to tell them how much he valued their performances. He used to write me a personal note every now and then just to tell me that he appreciated the work I was doing.

In all the years I have been in business, Ed Sullivan was the only client who ever sent me so many personal notes expressing his gratitude for my work. Sullivan often personally called performers, especially during the early days of the show, to ask them to appear on his program. In the first few years, Sullivan was really the principal booker and talent agent for the show.

4

A Complicated Man

In the world of television, Ed Sullivan was the ringmaster of the most successful weekly variety program in history. To his friends and relatives, Sullivan was an enigma, a contradiction of emotions and enormous drive that surfaced rarely in public. Bob Precht, his producer and son-in-law, was probably one of his closest companions, yet Precht admits that he often "never knew what Sullivan was thinking."

There is no doubt that Sullivan's wife, Sylvia, was his closest confidante, his constant companion at the numerous social and entertainment events he attended, the person he often looked to for approval and advice. Their marriage was a strong bond that lasted for over forty years, and they were seldom apart for more than a day or two during that union. After every television show, Sullivan would call Sylvia on the telephone from his dressing room to discuss the program. (Sylvia almost always watched the show in their apartment at the Delmonico, often with Ed and Sylvia's daughter, Betty Precht.) After the show the Sullivans and the Prechts would have a late supper together at a popular midtown restaurant such as Gino's or Danny's Hideaway.

The Sullivans were a close family even though Sylvia, born Sylvia Levine, was Jewish, and Ed Sullivan was a devoted Catholic for all of his life. (He even was elected to the Knights of Malta, a Catholic society that honored distinguished Catholic laymen.) It was not unusual for Sullivan to attend Mass at cathedrals and churches when

Ed Sullivan and his wife, Sylvia, at dinner at Danny's Hideaway
in the late 1940s. (Bernie Ilson)

he traveled to cities in the States and in Europe. I remember he asked me to accompany him on several of these visits (although I am not Catholic and Sullivan knew it).

I believe he invited me to accompany him because he did not want to leave me out of things.

He had a genuine interest in people and was more comfortable away from the stage of the Ed Sullivan Theater, where he never appeared at ease and, in fact, wasn't. Being on stage produced an anxiety in Ed Sullivan, while walking on the streets of New York City did not.

I believe he had a burning ambition to succeed and tried his best to hide it. And yet there was a mysterious side of him, a side that was concealed from most everyone and probably from himself. It erupted rarely, but when it did, the fighting Irishman appeared and he became the sportsman who could fiercely compete on the golf course; the columnist who fought his detractors (often rival newspaper columnists) with terse, caustic words; the moralist who dismissed Jackie Mason for an alleged offensive gesture on camera; the taskmaster who demanded performers and musicians appear on time and banished them from his stage if they appeared on a rival program.

There was a curtain, a sort of a veil that covered Sullivan's everyday persona, which lifted a bit when he was in the comfortable company of a fellow Irishman. It seemed as if Sullivan reverted to an earlier era when his Gaelic forebearers would relax in the comfort of a pub and talk about times past, long-gone relatives, meals of potatoes and soda bread, and the "damn" English.

This veil would vanish when he met Hal Boyle, a columnist for the Associated Press (AP), who would interview him now and then at my request. The interview would often take place in late afternoon in a corner of a pub near the AP offices at Rockefeller Center. Although I sat in at these meetings, I rarely said a word. I'd sip my tea and try to be part of the wallpaper as these older Irish gentlemen (they were both in their sixties at the time) would talk about anything that crossed their minds. The conversation often wandered from reminiscences about recently departed friends in the newspaper business, to where to eat, and on to the sorry state of the media world. Two topics were seldom discussed, politics and *The Ed Sullivan Show*, even though I had set up the meeting for Sullivan to discuss his newest bookings. Later, I sent Hal background information on the new attractions and his column would reflect my notes. I always thought he should have written about their conversations, but that seemed to be too "personal" for Hal, and he no doubt believed that their "small talk" would be of no interest to his thousands of readers.

Conversation did not flow easily between the two men. They would often sit there picking at their food, Sullivan slowly sipping his white wine (which he spiced with Sweet'n Low packets he always carried in his coat pocket) and Hal nursing a beer and a ham sandwich. Often they would stare at the food and hum a tune quietly, almost intelligibly. If one started humming, the other soon followed. Then suddenly, Hal would start the conversation anew with "Have you heard that Johnson is ailing again?"

"No," Ed would answer.

"Yes," Hal would offer. "I hear it's the gout."

"You don't say," Ed would answer.

"I do say," Hal would reply. "He's getting about with a cane now."

"If you see him, give him my best," Ed would say.

Then they would be silent for a few more minutes, and the humming would start again. I kept thinking the tune was "Danny Boy," but I could never quite identify it, because they both seemed to hum off-key. With Hal Boyle, Sullivan seemed content to just spend a quiet hour or so conversing about old friends and humming.

Ed Sullivan was never comfortable talking about the show. He knew the value of publicity probably better than any client I ever had, but he was obviously embarrassed about talking about himself and the show, especially with Hal Boyle. Perhaps this was because Sullivan always considered himself a newspaperman, not an entertainer, and it was difficult for him to discuss his role as showman with an old colleague such as Hal.

Nevertheless, when he was thrust into the role of spokesperson for the show, Sullivan knew how to promote it and needed no preliminary instructions about what to say. Being a veteran newspaperman, he understood what information the interviewer was seeking and laid it on with an air of enthusiasm; however, if credit were to be given for an innovative booking, Sullivan always gave the honor to his producer and the staff. The words "I did that" were never part of his conversation with an interviewer.

Sullivan preferred to walk the streets of New York alone, or with his wife or a friend. Sometimes he would say to me, "Let's take a walk, Bernard." And so I would walk with him back to his apartment at the Delmonico, situated about ten blocks from the Ed Sullivan Theater if you go directly, but on these walks he often diverted from a straight line back to the apartment to wander through Central Park. There was little talk between us about the show or about the news of the day. Instead Sullivan liked to point out the glories of nature in the park, the blooming daffodils, or a frisky dog. At other times, he'd invite me to have a shoeshine with him at his favorite shoeshine parlor on East 59th Street, or sometimes he would stop to have late lunch at Gino's and ask me to dine with him. Sullivan always had a piece of roast chicken with no sauce or dressing of any kind. He ate it with relish, often commenting it was one of the best chickens he ever had. Sometimes, he would take a leg of the chicken, wrap it up in a napkin, and put it in his pocket. He stashed it away so that he could nibble on it later if he got hungry. It appeared that he ate little, but often. I was to learn later that Sullivan's nasal passages had been injured when he took up boxing as a youth and damaged his taste buds.

Sometimes I met him for breakfast, which he usually took alone at Child's Restaurant, a medium-priced chain restaurant near his apartment. His breakfast was almost always the same: two baby lamb chops, well done.

I remember during one of our quiet lunches, I had been in a talkative mood and was prattling on about a show I had seen. Sullivan, mistaking it for an attempt to suggest a particular performer for his own show, suddenly put aside his chicken, looked me straight in the eye, and said, "Do you really mean that?" His light blue eyes were solidly fixed on mine, and the voice seemed to come from the depths of his soul. He obviously misinterpreted what I was saying. "Yes," I slowly answered. "I do believe that." At that moment, his eyes stared back at me for what seemed like an eternity, and then just as suddenly, he looked at his plate, picked at his chicken, and said, "Then talk to Bob Precht about it." For just a fleeting moment, I had seen the real Ed Sullivan suddenly come to life, a questioning Ed Sullivan, a skeptical Ed Sullivan, a wary Ed Sullivan, a man who was all business, and it was almost chilling.

When the Montreal Expo was announced in 1968, Bob Precht called me and suggested a meeting. It had been decided to present two shows directly from the Expo grounds, and he asked me to write a news release and prepare the press for the shows, which would be beamed live from the newest World's Fair and the first to be held in Canada. A few weeks later, I found myself working from an office on the Expo grounds and fielding calls from the foreign press for interviews with Ed Sullivan.

One of the calls came from the manager of the Russian exhibit at Expo. The Russians had built a giant-size pavilion for an exhibit that featured an Olympic-size pool filled with caviar-bearing sturgeon, a gallery of art illustrative of their technical accomplishments, and one of the best restaurants at the fair. The Russian manager explained that since Sullivan had originated more than half a dozen shows from Russia, visiting Moscow and Stalingrad, and had featured the Bolshoi Ballet, the Moiseyev Dancers, and the Moscow

Ed presented most of his shows "live" from the stage of the Ed Sullivan Theater on Broadway in New York City, but occasionally he traveled to exotic places to film interesting personalities and their work. In 1966, Ed traveled to Europe to interview director/actor John Huston on the set of the motion picture, *The Bible*. (Photofest)

Circus on his show, the Russian journalists were anxious to interview him. I checked with Sullivan and Bob Precht, who speaks Russian fluently, and they felt, as I did, that it would help future relations with the Russian bureaucrats in charge of the artistic exchange office. Precht did not have time to sit in on the interview. The Expo shows were complicated and were taking up all of his time. He asked if an interpreter would be necessary. I informed him that the Russians had explained that the interview would be conducted entirely in English and that the journalists would submit their questions in advance. Everything seemed to be routine.

The interview was set for lunch the following day, and the interview questions were supposed to be sent by messenger that morning. The questions never arrived. I called the manager of the Russian exhibit, who assured me the interview questions were on the way. I informed Sullivan and Precht about it and suggested that perhaps the interview should be postponed. Sullivan stepped in and said, "Let's just do it. I've dealt with the Russians before. They have been very good to the show." And so, Sullivan and I left for the lunch. I suggested an executive car (really just a fancy golf cart) that was available to us for moving about the fair, but Sullivan said, "It's a nice day. Let's walk."

I thought that was the first mistake.

The Russian pavilion was about four hundred yards from our office. As we started walking down the street, the people at the Expo began to recognize Ed Sullivan; at first it was just a glance or two, the kind of attention Sullivan received on his walks through the streets of New York, but soon fairgoers began to run up to him with cameras and autograph books and we were surrounded by a growing mob. Usually Sullivan would stop and sign autographs or pose for a picture or two, but it was impossible with this surging throng of humanity. After a few minutes, the Expo police arrived and "rescued" us from the autograph seekers. Sullivan took it in his stride, but I was shaken for a moment or two. I don't like crowds, especially if they are moving in my direction.

The Expo "gendarmes" put us in an executive cart and took us to the Russian pavilion where the manager and the journalists were at the entrance to greet us. I looked at the manager and his entourage and realized that instead of a few journalists, he had assembled almost all of the employees of the pavilion. We were escorted past the pool of swimming sturgeon to a private room in the back of the restaurant, which was set up with a sumptuous buffet of food and drink and featured half a dozen waiters and bartenders dressed in tuxedos. It wasn't to be just an interview. It was a party.

I thought that was mistake number two.

My instincts told me to take Sullivan by the arm and leave immediately, but I knew Sullivan wouldn't go. I looked at him and motioned that we should leave. Sullivan turned to me, knew what I was going to say, and whispered back. "It's going to be fine."

And so the party began.

The manager brought out several trays of caviar, obviously Beluga, "pearls" of the blackest, shiniest caviar I had ever seen. I tasted the delicacy, and it was as wonderful as expected. Immediately the fleet of waiters produced bottles of vodka, encased in ice, and set them up at our table. I noticed right away that the bottles had strange labels. There was no commercial name of a recognized Russian brand such as Stolichnaya. Instead, the labels were handwritten in a Russian scrawl, and I remember the ink was red. The manager picked up a bottle, announced, "Our best vodka," and offered a toast, "To America and *The Ed Sullivan Show*." He poured the liquid into iced shot glasses and handed it to Sullivan and me.

All of the entourage poured themselves vodka and lifted their small glasses. Sullivan responded, "To the Russian people and their great artists," and he drank it down in chug-a-lug style. I was amazed. I knew Sullivan had a problem with ulcers. I had never seen him drink hard liquor. I knew that Sullivan's usual drink was white wine spiked with Sweet'n Low, but here he was drinking vodka and eating caviar and obviously enjoying himself.

I must admit that this vodka, the vodka with the handwritten red label, was the best vodka I had ever tasted. It went down smooth and warm and produced a buzz just seconds later. The toasts went on and on. Food began to fill our table, smoked fish, more caviar (in a variety of colors), chicken, meats of all types. It was a feast, not a luncheon. After three vodkas, I began to feel tipsy and so I faked the rest of the toasts, but Sullivan must have downed six or seven vodkas and had eaten very little. I remember him picking at the chicken, but he just tasted the caviar. He seemed to be having a good time. When the toasts ceased, the journalists assembled in a row in front of us, and the interview commenced.

Since we did not have the questions in advance as promised, I took the manager of the pavilion aside and asked him for the questions. "What questions?" he replied.

"The questions for Mr. Sullivan. We were promised them in advance."

"I don't know who promised that," said the manager. "We always conduct our interviews spontaneously."

"Who have you interviewed," I asked.

The manager stopped and thought for a moment, then offered, "No one. Mr. Sullivan is our first interview."

I sensed what had happened and took Sullivan aside. "There are no advance questions as they promised. It looks like a setup," I told Sullivan. I suggested we leave.

Sullivan looked at me, shook his head, and said, "It's going to be all right. They're just newspapermen." He hesitated for a second and added, "And so am I."

I realized that the Russians had hoped to get Sullivan drunk and off balance. They were looking for a story about the show and obviously were intent on tricking a tipsy Sullivan into saying something embarrassing, but they did not get their wish.

During the entire interview, Sullivan was at his best. He parried questions like a boxer feinting with his left, and then hitting them with his right by constantly saying, "I admire the Russian people and want to thank you for sending your talented artists to appear on our show." He reminded them how they all had toasted the Bolshoi Ballet and the Moiseyev Dancers and other great Russian dancers, singers, and musicians who appeared on his show. "We, the American people, and you the Russian people, have a lot in common."

The amazing part of the interview was that it took place during the anxieties of the cold war, when the editorial pages were condemning Russia for its aggressive actions toward neighboring countries. And here was Sullivan lauding the Russian people and its artists, but being careful not to mention the Russian government, Stalin, or its politics. I have never seen a more skillful performance from Ed Sullivan, and to think it was after he consumed half a dozen potent vodkas.

Ed Sullivan was aware that he had handled the situation well, and as we left the Russian pavilion, he turned to me and said, "We showed them we can play their game, right?"

And then he added, "They are not real newspapermen. Just amateurs."

The executive cart was waiting for us at the curb, a smiling Ed Sullivan leading the way, and we returned to our base at the fair.

What I had thought would be a mistake, was not. I had just underestimated Sullivan's ability to size up a difficult situation and make it work for him. That incident was early in our relationship. After that occasion, I realized that Sullivan had a set of instincts that came into play when needed and could carry him through any rough situations with the media. He knew how to play the press game from both sides. I also discovered that he could drink with the best . . . if necessary.

Another aspect of Ed Sullivan's personality was his tendency to become so absorbed in the progress of the show that he occasionally forgot he was the ringmaster and became part of the audience or

As an extension of the U.S. State Department Cultural Exchange Program, Ed Sullivan devoted his entire program to the world-famous Moscow Circus on April 12, 1966. In this drawing by John Ryan, Ed is shaking hands with Popov, Russia's famed clown, as a friendly trained bear looks on. (Photofest)

even one of the participants. More than once, Ed Sullivan found himself at the top of a pyramid of acrobats as part of their finale. Ed and Bob felt that Ed's participation in an act helped humanize what some unkind critics called Ed's "great stone face." In later years, Ed even did sketches with some of the performers. In one, in which he appeared with Soupy Sales, Ed received one of Soupy's famous pies in the face. (The Soupy Sales "pies" were made of shaving cream over a thin pie crust.)

The appearance of Victor the Bear on the show is a good example. Everything went well during the rehearsal show. Victor balanced himself on a large ball, turned somersaults, and walked on a balance beam, all the time tethered by a leather loop on one of his legs and a loosely held chain that the trainer maneuvered as the big, brown six-foot bear went through its acrobatic routine.

The trainer explained to Bob Precht and Sullivan that Victor did his tricks because the bear knew that at the end of the act, he would be fed a large cone of ice cream, his favorite food. The trainer's wife held the ice cream cone just offstage, where Victor could see it as he went through his routine and gave it to the bear as he exited the stage. That is how it went during the afternoon rehearsal show.

The trainer suggested that perhaps during the actual show, Ed Sullivan could hold the ice cream cone while standing at the side of the stage where he and the ice cream cone were visible to the bear. At the close of the act, the trainer would take the cone from Ed and give it to Victor, drawing Ed into the picture, as Sullivan sometimes did with variety acts. Ed agreed to hold the ice cream cone and, that night during the actual show, in front of an audience of 35 million viewers, Victor the Bear and his trainer were introduced by Ed Sullivan and they moved to the center of the stage. As they did, the trainer handed Ed the ice cream cone.

The act began and Victor was in rare form. His tumbling was flawless; he scooted across the stage on a big red ball, and tiptoed across the balance beam, always watching Ed and the ice cream cone out of the corner of one eye.

Sullivan was captivated by Victor's performance, so much so, that he forgot he was the host of the show and became part of the audience. He momentarily became a kid again, a kid at the circus. As he watched the bear's performance, Sullivan began to slowly eat the ice cream cone. Victor immediately spotted this and his brain must have said to him, "Someone is eating my ice cream cone."

At that point, Victor hopped off the balance beam, broke across the stage dragging his chain and the trainer with him, stopped directly in front of Ed Sullivan, and in one sweep of his massive paw, swiped the cone from the stunned Sullivan. With cone in hand, Victor exited into the wings and proceeded to his dressing room, dragging the bewildered trainer behind him.

It could have been a tragedy. The bear could have taken Ed Sullivan's arm off as he retrieved his cone. But luckily, Victor was only interested in ice cream, not human beings. Unfortunately, the bear's confrontation with Ed Sullivan was not recorded on camera, because the camera moves had been programmed in advance, and there was no camera on Sullivan during this part of the act.

Sullivan, a bit shaken by the experience, instinctively knew what to do. He stepped forward and, facing the camera, said, "And thank you, Victor the Bear, for that remarkable performance."

5

The Columnist and His Competition

During the entire run of *The Ed Sullivan Show*, Sullivan continued to write his column for the *New York Daily News/Chicago Tribune* Syndicate three times a week. He was aided by his longtime assistant, Carmine Santullo, who helped Sullivan gather items for the column from news sources and press agents. Sullivan would also use his own set of notes on these entertainment events to make comments in his peppery, breezy style. These notes were the framework for his next column. He typed the final version of each column on his gold-plated portable typewriter at a small desk in the living room of his apartment.

In today's world of television and the Internet, it may be difficult to imagine the great impact that the plethora of gossip columns had on the public in the 1930s, '40s, and '50s. The columnist was the "king" of the entertainment world and columns were read by everyone for entertainment and information. The public read Winchell and Sullivan to find out who was "hot," who was fading, whose career was soaring, who was dating who, who was divorcing who, and who was headed up to the altar with whom.

From the 1920s to the beginning of the 1950s, the number one columnist was certainly Walter Winchell. Coming up second to Winchell was Ed Sullivan. Though Winchell was the "top dog" in the world of gossip columnists for decades, that all changed with the advent of television. Eventually, Ed Sullivan's fame and power far outdistanced Winchell's after the success of *The Ed Sullivan Show*.

Winchell's column appeared in the *New York Daily Mirror* and the other papers in the Hearst newspaper chain, as well as in scores of independent newspapers all over the country, but Winchell and Sullivan also had competition from more than a dozen other gossip columnists.

The other popular columnists were Dorothy Kilgallen, Louis Sobol, and Bert Bacharach,[1] writing in the *New York Journal American* and other Hearst newspapers, while Leonard Lyons, Sidney Skolsky, and Earl Wilson were writing for the *New York Post*. In addition to Ed Sullivan, the *New York Daily News* featured columnists Danton Walker and Bob Sylvester. Frank Farrell's column appeared in the *New York World Telegram*. Chicago's lone entry was Irv Kupcinet, who wrote for the *Chicago Sun Times* and was widely syndicated.

Ed Sullivan and Walter Winchell. (Photofest)

In Los Angeles, the columns were almost exclusively concerned with the movie industry. The two queens of the columnists on the West Coast were Louella Parsons, the doyenne of the Hearst newspaper empire, and Hedda Hopper, the Hollywood columnist for the *Chicago Tribune* Syndicate. These ladies concentrated on gossip about movie stars and the picture business, as did *Daily Variety* and the *Hollywood Reporter*, which were called "trade papers" and covered the gossip, news, and business decisions of the film business.

Ironically, there is more interest in show business gossip today than there ever was in the heyday of Winchell and Sullivan, but the impact on the public is not nearly as powerful. If Winchell awarded an entertainer "an orchid" for a performance in a film or mentioned that a singer's new recording looked like a hit, it meant thousands in sales for that lucky performer. Today, a story in the *National Enquirer* or the *Star* or any supermarket publication has no real impact on sales of movie tickets, CDs, or books. A short paragraph in page 6 in the *New York Post* or an item in Liz Smith's column might stir up a little interest in a new book, but in today's media market, only an appearance on *Oprah* could produce fifty thousand instant sales for a new book and be a step up to inclusion in the *New York Times*'s Best Sellers list. Television has become the medium of choice for marketing movies, CDs, DVDs, books, or sports events and concerts. Gossip columns have become just "entertainment," to be read for the fun of knowing what Brad Pitt or Madonna are doing, so that you are "in the know" at the office water cooler or the country club.

Times have changed. Publicists used to seek out Winchell at his favorite table at the Stork Club or try to trap Leonard Lyons on his nightly prowl among the nightclubs and restaurants of the Broadway crowd. Instead, the public relations counselors (no longer called press agents or flacks) arrange for their clients to appear on

The Today Show; *Good Morning, America*; *The Tonight Show with Jay Leno*; *The Late Show with David Letterman*; *Entertainment Tonight*; *Access Hollywood*; *The Larry King Show*; *Live with Regis and Kelly*; *Ellen*; and a dozen other "talk" or magazine-type television shows where the impact is much greater than any newspaper column.

In early 1965, I asked Ed if he had a short piece he had written from his career as a sports writer. I felt that it would make an interesting piece to have on hand as part of *The Ed Sullivan Show* press kit. Ed went through his files and came up with the following article:

Many years ago, I had an experience which to this very day stands out in my mind most vividly. It involved one of my personal heroes, Babe Ruth, perhaps the most colorful American sports figure of all time. And it involved an event that is still discussed and argued about by fans and baseball historians.

Back in the early days of my career as a newspaperman, I was a sports reporter before I started covering the Broadway beat. I worked for the old *New York Graphic* then as a baseball writer. It was 1932 and I was in Chicago for the third game of the World Series between the New York Yankees and the Chicago Cubs. The Yankees had already taken two games and were looking for a clean sweep of the series.

I got out to Wrigley Field early and to save time started writing the lead to my story. I guess I got carried away by the excitement of covering the Series, and started typing at a furious pace. The words poured out and I was writing without thinking. And then I stopped to check the story.

I was stunned—for I had written that Babe Ruth had smashed a home run in the fifth inning. And I had written that before the game started. Well, I scrapped the story.

The game started and went along until the fifth inning—and

then Babe Ruth came to bat. The Chicago fans had been on him all during the game. This time he stepped up to the plate and after a couple of swings, he stepped out in front and made that now-famous gesture of pointing toward the stands, as if to indicate that he would send the next pitch into the seats for a home run.

Well—that's exactly what he did. And, with a shock I remembered what I had written earlier. As the Babe trotted around the bases, I dug down into my pocket for the crumpled sheets of paper that had been my story. Sure enough—here it was . . . Babe hitting a homer in the fifth.

That was more than thirty years ago. Today, the argument still continues whether he actually made that gesture. But for me, of course, what I remember most of the '32 Series are those words I wrote.

Ultimately, the article was never added to our press kit, because Ed did not want to rekindle his past accomplishments. His entire attention, he said, was the promotion of what would be on next week on *The Ed Sullivan Show.*

6
Elvis Presley, the Highest Paid Sullivan Guest

n 1956, Ed Sullivan signed Elvis Presley to appear on his show for three appearances for a fee of fifty thousand dollars, which was more than he had ever paid a performer. At the time, Presley was the hottest star in the show business galaxy.

It had been established, at that time, that the maximum salary for an appearance on *The Ed Sullivan Show* by a top-rung entertainer like Bing Crosby or Frank Sinatra was $7,500. Presley's records were topping the charts and his concerts at a theater or even a thirty-thousand-seat stadium were sold-out appearances.

Colonel Tom Parker, Presley's manager and, in fact, his partner who pocketed 50 percent of Presley's earnings, was a hard bargainer and knew Sullivan needed Presley to appear on his show to battle his 1956 adversary, *The Steve Allen Show* on NBC.

Only a few weeks earlier, Presley had appeared on *The Steve Allen Show*, and it helped Allen win the ratings war for the week over *The Ed Sullivan Show*, a rare occurrence. It was a situation that Sullivan knew he had to remedy. Elvis Presley's first and second appearances on *The Ed Sullivan Show* enabled it to soar in the Nielsen ratings, and Sullivan handily beat all the competition. However, Presley's performance also drew a barrel-full of indignant letters from Sullivan's audience protesting Presley's hip gyrations and provocative leg movements and a torrent of critical comment from straight-laced newspaper columnists. Sullivan, ever the showman, but also the purveyor of "clean, or rather spotless" entertainment, knew he had to find a solution to this dilemma of criticism. He came up with a photographic answer. In Presley's third appearance on January 6, 1957, the cameramen on *The Ed Sullivan Show* photographed Presley only from the waist up. There were no shots of his moving torso. In fact, the cameramen were instructed to keep the cameras rigidly in place, as if they were shooting a painting. It worked. The audience wrote no more disparaging letters, and the columnists sought new targets for their diatribes.

It is an interesting footnote that Ed Sullivan did not introduce Elvis Presley in his first appearance on the show. On August 5, 1956, Sullivan had been seriously injured in a car accident in Connecticut, and Charles Laughton took over as the substitute host of *The Ed Sullivan Show* for Presley's first performance. Laughton,

Elvis Presley. (Photofest)

apparently catching "Sullivanitis," the mispronouncing of an entertainer's name, introduced the singer as "Elvin" Presley.

In a strange way, Presley's appearances on the Sullivan show not only helped Elvis Presley's career and moved him in the direction of motion pictures and Hollywood, but they also resulted in a cameo role for Ed Sullivan in the feature motion picture *Bye Bye Birdie*, the big-screen version of the Broadway hit starring Dick Van Dyke. The story line of this musical had Conrad Birdie, an obvious carbon copy of Elvis, enlist in the Army and give his last civilian kiss to a girl on the stage of *The Ed Sullivan Show*. To set this scene in the Broadway show (and later the motion picture), the songwriters, Strouse and Adams, wrote a special song, "A Hymn to Ed Sullivan," which was sung in the show (and later the movie) by comedian Paul Lynde. The song ends with the line, "We love you Ed Sullivan." Sullivan, in an atypical gesture, agreed to play himself in the movie version, and it marked Ed Sullivan's only appearance as the host of his show in a Hollywood film.

Sullivan told the press and later his audience that Elvis Presley was a "fine, decent young man" and that he was delighted to have Elvis on the show. Sullivan had been informed that at a CBS press conference, a newspaperman had chided Presley for having a following of "silly young girls who even planted kisses on his pink Cadillac." Presley replied, "Well, sir, if it weren't for those silly young girls I wouldn't have a Cadillac," to which Sullivan commented, "That kid is going to go places." And he certainly did.

I personally had an impromptu meeting with the future star in 1953, when I met Elvis Presley in the waiting room of the William Morris Agency. I had an appointment with Jerry Collins, who was then the publicity director of the famous talent agency. I asked him who he was waiting to see and he said, "No one, sir, I am jus' waitin' for my manager. He's meeting with Mr. Kalcheim."

"What do you do?" I asked.

"I sing and play the geetah," Presley replied.

"Where have you worked?"

"Mostly in the South, in clubs and fairs. I'm going to make a few records soon."

"For what record company?"

"I think it is called Sun Records," he said, smiling. "I like the name Sun. Don't you?"

"I know the company. They are in the country and western field."

"Yeh, that's what I sing. Country songs."

"Well, good luck," I said, and went off to meet Jerry Collins.

Little did I know, that three years later, this tall, smiling country boy would be the hottest singing talent in the business. So I left him waiting for Colonel Parker to finish his meeting with Harry Kalcheim, one of the most important agents at the William Morris Agency. I mentioned the name Elvis Presley to Jerry Collins at our meeting, and he said, "Never heard of him. He can't be an important client."

Years later when I mentioned to Jerry this conversation we had about Elvis, he said that at the time he was right. The "country music craze" didn't hit the entertainment industry until years later, but Presley led the way. Until Presley and Colonel Parker came onto the scene, country music (at the time called country and western music) was a regional phenomenon. There had been many country artists, such as Hank Williams and Eddy Arnold, who had made a greater impact on the music scene, but it was not until Elvis, who became the first big "crossover" artist (a performer who achieves success in more than one genre), that country music had a nationwide impact.

7
Ed Meets the Beatles

Articles on *The Ed Sullivan Show* inevitably mention the Beatles' and Elvis Presley's appearances on the program as highlights of the series. When the Beatles first appeared on *The Ed Sullivan Show*, they attracted the largest audience for an entertainment program to that date, more than 73 million viewers. More than forty years later, the pop icons still exert a potent influence on music and the buying public of America.

Their appearance on the show further reinforces Ed Sullivan's ability to anticipate and, in a sense, create a focus on an entertainment phenomenon and present it to the American public.

Sometimes it is luck, chance, or happenstance that makes a difference in your success. You can do all the right things, and still, if luck is against you, the result will not be a happy one. In 1964, my life crossed paths with the Beatles. They were signed to appear on the program, and I was the press representative for the show and for Sullivan Productions. I made all the right moves. I contacted the press, and I beat the drum telling the world that the Beatles were on their way to America. At the time, however, the Beatles were virtually unknown in the States. I could not get the media excited about this unknown British singing group with a funny name.

That was when luck came my way.

Here is an excerpt of an article I wrote for *Total Magazine* in 1989 about the event: "Is it possible that 25 years have passed since the Beatles burst into the national spotlight on *The Ed Sullivan*

Ed on stage with the Beatles (Paul, John, George, and Ringo). (Photofest)

Show? A record audience of 73 million viewers watched the Liverpool Four sing 'I Want to Hold Your Hand' as the live audience of 700 teenagers, mostly girls, screeched and swooned in their seats. In aisle seats, Leonard Bernstein and his wife, TV actress Felicia Montealegre, applauded the musical antics of the Beatles, whose appearance as a new show-business phenomenon was accepted by the mass and the 'class.' "[1]

The night was Sunday, February 9, 1964, and it was a triumphant one for the Fab Four and their manager, Brian Epstein. The American debut of the Beatles had been engineered personally by Ed Sullivan during a visit to England in November 1963. When Sullivan and his wife, Sylvia, landed at Heathrow Airport on one of their many talent-hunting trips, they were inadvertently surrounded by a surging throng of teenagers. There were ten thousand young women packed into the terminal, all in a state of joyous agitation, screaming the names of John, Paul, George, and Ringo. Sullivan soon discovered that the teenyboppers had come to the airport to greet the Beatles on their return from a German concert tour. "I thought, at first, that Elvis or the Queen had arrived," Sullivan later recalled, "but found it was the Beatles. I had never heard of the Beatles until then."

Although the Beatles had not had a hit record in America, Sullivan felt that their success in Great Britain and Europe could be transported to America. How could you not be influenced by ten thousand delirious teenagers? Sullivan, always a great believer in the ability of an audience to discover its own stars, felt that the young British fans must have seen something special in the songs of these long-haired kids from Liverpool. Sullivan offered Brian Epstein, the Beatles' manager, a contract for three appearances on the show for a total fee of $8,500. Epstein, who had been anxiously seeking an important television appearance to break through to the vast American audience, gladly accepted the offer. It was undoubtedly the best deal Sullivan ever negotiated.

At this point, I entered the picture. Sullivan sent me a telegram reading, "Just signed the Beatles, start publicity." I remembered that an article had been written about the Beatles in the *New York Times Magazine*, but it had been buried in the back pages among the classified advertisements. I was able to dig up a copy of the article. I also obtained some background material from Capitol Records, who had the Beatles under contract and had issued some of their records, but the information was lacking. I then informed Capitol about the Sullivan show's booking, and it was like hitting a horse with a razor-sharp spur. They were off and running. Word went out to their sales and record promotion departments to "push" the Beatles. I contacted the entertainment editors of the major magazines, which at the time were *Life*, *Look*, *Time*, and

Newsweek, but they didn't bite at the suggestion to do an article on an "unknown British rock group." I convinced several television columnists and music writers to interview the Beatles when they arrived in America, but it was thin pickings. Most writers were not interested. Jack Paar, who was also alert to new talent, heard about the Beatles and arranged to get a tape of a Beatles' performance for his late-night show. He knew of Sullivan's booking, so he jumped the gun and played the tape on his show in early January. But he made a monumental mistake. Paar played the spot for laughs instead of presenting them as an exciting, innovative new band that had become the hottest group in Great Britain, and, as a result, Paar's taped appearance fell flat.

A serendipitous occurrence helped to spark the campaign to

Bernie Ilson (center) backstage with Paul McCartney
and George Harrison. (Sullivan Productions)

publicize the appearance of the Beatles on *The Ed Sullivan Show*. On a Saturday morning in early January, George Hunt Jr., the editor of *Life* magazine, was driving in his car with his teenage daughter. She was listening to the radio as they traveled on a side road in suburban Westchester. Just as they went through a number of underpasses, the radio cut out. "Please, Dad," the daughter begged. "Stop the car. I'm missing the Beatles." Hunt complied and pulled over to the side of the road. His daughter rejoiced at the return of the music.

"Who are the Beatles?" Hunt asked.

"The best group around," his daughter answered. "All the kids at school are just crazy about the Beatles."

That was enough for the editor.

When he arrived at his office on Monday, his first call of the day was to his entertainment editor (Tommy Thompson) of whom he asked, "Why aren't we doing a piece on the Beatles?" Five minutes later the entertainment editor called me and said, "We've decided to do an article on that group you've been pitching to me. Where can we shoot them?"

I knew the Beatles were at the Olympia Theater in Paris and told him so.

"Good," he said. "Tell them we're flying over a team to shoot them." I contacted Brian Epstein and worked out the details.

The next week, the Beatles were featured in a five-page layout in *Life*. The article was the spark that ignited the rest of the press. That day my phone started ringing with requests to interview the group. It seemed as if everyone in the press wanted to talk to the Beatles. Disc jockeys began to play their music all day long. It was an avalanche of publicity. By the time the Beatles arrived, we had to use the ballroom of the Plaza Hotel to conduct the interviews with literally hundreds of members of the press. Dozens of New York policemen were assigned to encircle the Plaza Hotel, where the Beatles were staying, as well as the Ed Sullivan Theater on Broadway, where they were rehearsing for the show. It was a press agent's dream.

And it all happened because Ed Sullivan and the Beatles converged at Heathrow Airport at the same time.

If the editor of *Life* magazine had not been driving down a Westchester road with his teenage daughter, the Beatles' early success, and the success of my publicity campaign, might have failed. Of course, the Beatles would have eventually made it big in America, regardless. The talent was there, and their appeal and great recordings would have brought them to the top in time. But again, who can say for sure that luck had not played a role in this case?

Sullivan and Bob Precht knew instantly that they were sitting on the hottest performers in show business. They decided that after the success of the Beatles first record-breaking appearance on Sunday, February 9, that they should appear again the following week when the program was scheduled to originate live (as always) from the Deauville Hotel in Miami Beach. Since the Beatles' schedule permitted them to appear on the Miami Beach show, and since Sullivan's contract with the lads from Liverpool was for three appearances (with no specific dates agreed upon), an action plan for their second show was formulated.

I was dispatched to Miami International Airport to meet with their officials. Thousands of teenagers had turned New York's La Guardia Airport into a sea of screaming youngsters when the Beatles flew in from Great Britain the week before, and I wanted to make certain that the security personnel at Miami International were prepared for the same possibility. I described to them the melee that had occurred at La Guardia, and how we hoped we could avert such a situation in Miami. I was surprised to hear the head of security assure me that nothing like that would happen in Miami.

"Don't worry, young man," the head of security assured me.

"We have very tight security here. We have handled all kinds of celebrities, and never had a problem." It was a very short meeting. It was apparent to me that the Miami airport people had no idea of the tremendous appeal of the Beatles. Nor did they realize that the Sullivan show had announced that the Beatles were flying to Miami for a second program. Disc jockeys all over Florida had been playing the Beatles records and giving the teenagers information about when the Beatles would be arriving in Miami. I called the Sullivan office and informed them of my meeting and of the lackadaisical attitude of the security officials at the airport.

Since I knew the Sullivan party was arriving on a private plane, I suggested that they delay the plane from coming directly to the terminal, hold the plane on the tarmac, and not bring it into the airport proper. I told them that I would arrange for limousines to pick up the Beatles on the airfield. I called a local security agency and arranged to have a dozen of our own security people at the airport to guard the limousines. Of course, I informed the Miami airport officials of what I was doing. They thought I was crazy to worry about security, but did not interfere with our plans.

The day the Beatles were scheduled to arrive, fans began arriving at the airport in droves. At first, they were just noisy, but as the crowd of teenagers grew and grew, shouts of "Where are the Beatles?" filled the terminal, and the kids crowded together like canned sardines. Growing into an angry mob of youngsters, they surged against the exit doors to the airfield. Sensing a growing disaster, I rushed outside and raced across the tarmac to our line of limousines. As the crowd realized the Beatles' plane had landed, they broke through the doors of the terminal and ran onto the field. Our limousines were lined up at the edge of the field, and I quickly jumped into the lead limo. I told the driver to head directly toward the plane, which was, by now, slowly taxiing toward the terminal. As the aircraft came to a halt, the lead limousine moved up to the airplane. The door of the aircraft opened, and the metal stairs slid down in front of the first limousine. Out came the Beatles, rushing down the steps. I guided them into the lead limousine.

Less than one hundred yards away, the teen mob (it was no longer just "a crowd of noisy kids") raced toward the limousines. I got quickly into the second limousine with the Sullivan staff, and we raced off toward the Miami Beach Causeway.

The Deauville Hotel is in Miami Beach, which is connected to the city of Miami by a series of low-slung roadways and bridges called causeways. To reach the Deauville Hotel, it was necessary to use the causeway, which has only three lanes in each direction. It is usually a very busy thoroughfare. As the limousines sped across the causeway, Beatles fans in hot-rod autos and motorcycles raced to catch up with us, forming a motorized escort of enthusiastic teenagers. Some of the fans leaned out from the hot rods with autograph books extended toward the limos, begging for the Beatles' autographs. It was a surrealistic scene. Finally, a contingent of Miami motorcycle police officers caught up with the speeding caravan of limousines and hot rods and dispersed the wild-eyed fans. I realized quickly that there were Miami television newsmen and cameramen along with the hot-rodders. That night the stations reported the airport event and the causeway ride on their programs. The media coverage increased day by day. The Miami media and hundreds of national and international media soon camped outside the Deauville Hotel to cover the Beatles invasion.

Life magazine sent two photographers and a reporter to do a follow-up story, and the following week photographs of the Beatles frolicking in the pool and rehearsing for *The Ed Sullivan Show* appeared in the country's most popular magazine. But that was only the tip of the iceberg. There were pictures and stories in just about every magazine that covered the entertainment scene. It was an avalanche of publicity.

Sullivan had expected to space the Beatles' three appearances on his show by at least a few weeks, but when you are riding a winning horse, you don't let go of the reins. So Sullivan decided that the Beatles third appearance on his show would be on the following Sunday, February 23, 1964. Unfortunately, the Beatles had already been booked into a theater in Europe and could not appear "live." Sullivan and Bob Precht filmed the Beatles singing three new songs, and that film was used on the following week. In all, the Beatles would be seen ten times on *The Ed Sullivan Show* over the next six years, and only four of them were "live" appearances.

By appearing on *The Ed Sullivan Show* in 1964, the Beatles opened the door for the British invasion of "rock groups." Although Sullivan was not a great fan of rock 'n' roll music, he was wise enough to book such acts on his show. Sullivan brought the Rolling Stones, the Animals, the Dave Clark Five, Herman's Hermits, and other U.K. groups to the attention of the television public, and was a definite factor in the British invasion during the latter part of the 1960s.

There is an interesting sidelight to the first Beatles show that came to my attention when the comedy team of Charley Brill and Mitzi McCall appeared on *This American Life*, a weekly radio program on Chicago Public Radio that aired February 21, 2005. The theme of this particular program was "My Big Break."

The "break" for this comedy team directly relates to Brill and McCall's appearance on *The Ed Sullivan Show* on February 9, 1964. Brill and McCall, a husband and wife duo (who are still married), had been successfully moving ahead with their comedy career. They had been appearing at nightclubs in Los Angeles, New York, and Las Vegas, and had a well-known manager named Mace Newfeld. In December 1963, Mace called Brill and McCall and gave them the good news that he had booked them for an appearance on *The Ed Sullivan Show* for February 9. The comedy team was over-

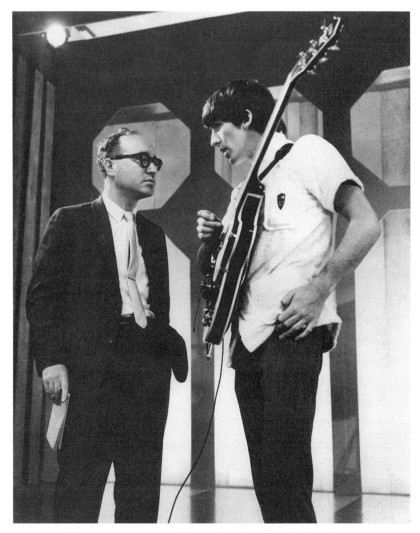

George Harrison conferring with Bernie Ilson backstage. (Sullivan Productions)

joyed at the news because, at that time, appearing on Sullivan's show was the most important television showcase for an upcoming comedy act. It was like appearing on Johnny Carson's *Tonight Show* in the 1970s or '80s or performing on *The Tonight Show with Jay Leno* or David Letterman's *Late Show* today.

When Brill and McCall arrived at CBS Studio 50 for the rehearsal of the show (the theater was not renamed the Ed Sullivan Theater until 1967), they were amazed to see the block around the theater was cordoned off by the police, and thousands of young girls were standing and shouting from behind the barricades. Brill and McCall made their way to the stage entrance and were assigned to a dressing room on the third floor, which was obviously not the star's dressing room, because, in addition to a dressing table and a few chairs, there was a large Coca-Cola machine. They were also surprised to find out that there would be a full audience for the rehearsal show and that the show's running order would be the same as the actual telecast. Brill and McCall decided that instead of revealing the punch lines of their jokes at the rehearsal show, they would just say, "blah, blah, blah." They reasoned that if they revealed the punch lines, they would not get the laughs from the band and the stage crew.

Brill and McCall began to get the idea that there was something special and unusual about that week's show when Sullivan opened the program with a musical act they had never heard of. When Sullivan announced, "And here they are, the Beatles," the roar from the audience was tremendous. Charley Brill remembers, "I could not hear them singing. The noise from the audience was deafening and did not stop until the group left the stage."

Brill and McCall were not aware of the tremendous popularity of the Beatles with teenagers. The duo had not noticed the enormous wave of publicity or the constant radio play of Beatles' records preceding the group's scheduled appearance on *The Ed Sullivan Show*. When Brill and McCall were initially booked on the show, they discovered that Frank Gorshin, a famous comedy impressionist, would also be on the program, and they assumed that he was the headline act. Also on the bill was Tessie O'Shea, a British music hall singer, and a youngster named Davey Jones, who was appearing on Broadway in *Oliver!* and would sing a song from it, "I'd Do Anything." (Two years later, Davey would be starring on the television series *The Monkees*, a Beatles knockoff, and singing with the group on their hit recordings.)

Brill and McCall still did not understand the importance of the rehearsal show, nor that Sullivan and Bob Precht pruned it for the telecast according to the reactions of the rehearsal show audience. As they had planned, Brill and McCall did their act, and when it came time for the punch lines, Mitzi or Charley would say just, "Blah, blah, blah." The audience reaction to their turn was terrible. Very few laughs. Brill and McCall returned to their dressing room and began to realize that perhaps the elimination of the punch lines was a mistake. As soon as the show was over, a stern voice over the intercom announced, "Brill and McCall, please report to Ed Sullivan's dressing room."

Ed Sullivan was seated at his dressing table and immediately told them, "Your material is too sophisticated for these youngsters, and we are going to have the same type of young audience for the eight o'clock show. And what was this 'blah, blah, blah' business?"

Brill and McCall explained that they did not want to reveal the punch lines at the rehearsal show. Sullivan asked the team, "Didn't your agent explain how our show works? The rehearsal is a 'dress rehearsal' just like a Broadway show." And then he added, "Maybe we can save your spot. Let's see your whole act."

In Ed Sullivan's dressing room, Brill and McCall went through their entire nightclub act, all fifty minutes of their sketches and bits. Sullivan took notes as they worked and when they finished, he said, "Do the sketch about the audition for the film director and keep it under three minutes. And no 'blah, blah, blahs.'"

Brill and McCall returned to their dressing room realizing that in the next few hours, they had to rewrite their whole act. While they were working on the lines, there was a knock at the door. A young man entered and asked if he could get a soda from the machine. He approached the machine and realized it required payment. He asked, "Do you have a coin? I don't have any money." Brill took out a quarter and inserted it in the coin slot. A bottle of Coke dropped down, and Brill gave it to the young man. Obviously not realizing that the room was Brill and McCall's dressing room, the young man sat down to drink his soda pop. He produced a drawing pad and commenced to draw sketches of the comedy team and the Coke machine. After about ten minutes, the young man left and Brill and McCall continued to work on the routine.

By showtime, their new routine was finished and rehearsed, and at about 8:35, they were summoned to the stage. Neither Mitzi nor Charley remembers their act clearly. They felt there were few laughs and that they had "bombed." After their act, they waited for Ed Sullivan to call them over to his side of the stage, which was an indication that he liked their performance. But Sullivan never gave them the approving wave of his hand, and the comedy team retreated to their dressing room. Brill and McCall felt that they had messed up their "big break." Afterward, Frank Gorshin, a longtime friend, took them for a late dinner at Sardi's Restaurant, and tried to assure them they did "fine." However, their agent did not call them for six months.

The Ed Sullivan Show was not the end of the line for the comedy team. They returned to working nightclubs, and in Las Vegas they appeared as the opening act for their friend Ann-Margret.

Throughout the 1960s and '70s and into the '80s, Brill and Mc-Call worked steadily in nightclubs and television, eventually appearing on *The Tonight Show Starring Johnny Carson* six times. Some years later, they saw a tape of their performance on *The Ed Sullivan Show* and realized that they weren't as bad as they imagined. In fact, they did get a few laughs and a round of applause. They also discovered that when they told friends and fellow comedians about their appearance on the Sullivan show, everyone seemed impressed that they appeared with the Beatles on the group's very first television show in America. So in a way, it was a big break, but to their dismay, they never appeared on *The Ed Sullivan Show* again.

Incidentally, Brill and McCall later realized that the young man who had come to their dressing room for a soda pop, and stayed to sketch them, was John Lennon.

8

Mr. Sullivan Goes to Washington

Occasionally, Ed Sullivan would accept an invitation to visit another city as part of the publicity for the show or a project such as a new Ed Sullivan LP record. One such visit occurred in 1964 when he was promoting *Ed Sullivan's Favorite Irish Songs*, a new LP. Garfinckel's, a large department store in Washington, DC, had contacted the Sullivan office and suggested that he visit the store to promote the new LP. They offered to cover all expenses for the trip (which they shared, of course, with the record company). Sullivan usually turned down these offers, but he accepted this one, because I had mentioned to Ed that we were in contact with the White House. Lady Bird Johnson, the president's wife, had indicated through her spokesperson that she would enjoy having tea with Mr. Sullivan at the White House. I followed up with Mrs. Johnson's press person, who told me that Mrs. Johnson was a fan of *The Ed Sullivan Show* and that she and the president regularly watched the program. The press person and I arranged for Ed to have tea with Lady Bird following his appearance at the department store.

Unlike many celebrities, Ed Sullivan did not like traveling with an entourage. Since I had set up the trip, he suggested that I accompany him, but no one else. We arrived at the Washington airport at noon and were met by a representative from the department store, who whisked us to the store for Sullivan's appearance. There were about three hundred Sullivan fans in the department store's "Little

Theater," which is reserved for celebrity appearances. Sullivan gave a short speech about the songs that were selected for the recording, noting that his favorite tune was "Galway Bay." He then sat down at a desk prepared to autograph copies of the LP.

Sullivan was patient and gracious with his fans and asked each person's name so that he could personalize his autograph. It was then that the department store's publicity man called me aside and told me that I was wanted on the phone. It was a call from the White House. The voice on the other end of the phone said, "I am sorry, Mr. Ilson, but Mrs. Johnson will be unable to meet with Mr. Sullivan for tea. She was just informed about a problem at the ranch, and she had to leave for Texas just a few minutes ago."

"That's too bad," I replied, "Mr. Sullivan had been looking forward to meeting Mrs. Johnson." I have a reputation for visualizing good PR situations, and it kicked in at that moment. I asked the voice on the phone, "Would the president like to meet Ed Sullivan?"

The voice apparently turned away from the phone, but I could distinctly hear the voice call out, "Lyndon, would you like to meet Ed Sullivan?" There was a pause of about ten seconds. The voice came back on the phone. "The president would be glad to meet Mr. Sullivan. Please come to the White House at four o'clock. I will turn you over to my associate who will give you directions to the East Entrance."

That was it. The president and Ed Sullivan were to meet in two hours. I informed Sullivan of the change of plans, and he was obviously delighted. I asked the Garfinckel's PR man to come with us, since he had been to the White House before with visiting celebrities.

We were driven to the side entrance of the White House, had our credentials checked, and were ushered up to a large waiting room on the second floor. An assistant to the president told us that President Johnson was in a meeting and would meet with Mr. Sullivan in a few minutes. He then suggested, "Would you like to take a quick tour of the West Wing?"

Naturally, we accepted and followed the assistant into a set of offices that contained few workers but yards of files. "Most of the staffers have left for the day," offered the assistant. Everything looked very conventional, but there were well-dressed men in dark suits at every turn. These men were obviously Secret Service officers assigned to guard the president.

At the end of the corridor, the assistant announced, "This is the Cabinet Room."

We entered a room that must have been eighty feet long. A long, massive table dominated the room, and leather-lined chairs abutted the table on each side. Along the walls were additional rows of these tall dark chairs. There were at least one hundred chairs in the room. At the center of the table was one throne-like chair. It was taller and wider than all the other chairs and was obviously the president's chair. The assistant walked us around the room, pointing out special chairs such as the ones for the secretary of state and the secretary of defense. He finally paused behind the president's chair. The famous "red phone," with a direct line to the Kremlin, was on a little platform, slightly below the tabletop on the president's right. To the left of the chair, and unseen unless you are in the president's chair, was a series of small levers. The levers all had labels, each with the name of an assistant or secretary. There were also levers marked "Dr. Pepper," "Sprite," and "ice water." These were obviously the president's choice of beverages. The assistant motioned for us to move on, and we returned to the green waiting room.

Within a few minutes, the assistant returned and said, "Mr. Sullivan, please follow me. The president is anxious to meet you." Sullivan left and the Garfinckel's PR man and I settled back in our chairs. Just a few minutes later, the assistant came back and said,

"The president would like to meet you two gentlemen. Please follow me." I was delighted to be asked to meet the president, but I knew the invitation was spurred by a suggestion from Sullivan. Every time we went on a publicity junket, Sullivan made certain that I was part of the party. He always introduced me as his "associate," never as his press representative.

As we entered the Oval Office, I was impressed by the size of the room. It was much larger than I expected. The president and Sullivan were standing in front of the president's desk and Sullivan motioned for me to come close. The president extended his hand and I shook it. It was a surprisingly soft hand, and his grip was very gentle. President Johnson was a tall man, easily six foot three, and since I am five foot five, he bent over slightly as he shook my hand. The meeting took place during the last year of President Johnson's presidency, and he looked to me to be a tired man. His blue eyes looked a bit clouded, and his face was deeply lined, but his voice was strong and southern.

There were several flashes from cameras, and it was then that I noticed three photographers stationed across the large room. There was a cameraman shooting motion picture film, and two still photographers, both with a large selection of cameras on a table nearby. The photographers shot constantly during the meeting, sometimes with a flash, but mostly without it. There was little need for additional light, since the drapes were all pulled aside and light streamed in from the rose garden, just outside the glass doors. (A few weeks later, I received a selection of photographs from the meeting, one of which was personally autographed to me by the president.)

President Johnson took the lead in his conversation with Ed Sullivan, but the dialogue was so conventional that it would probably have been rejected as a script for a play or television show.

"I am so glad to meet you, Mr. Sullivan. I try to watch your program every Sunday," said the president.

Bernie Ilson, Ed Sullivan, and President Lyndon Johnson
in the White House Oval Office. (Bernie Ilson)

"I want to tell you that I think you are doing a great job," answered Sullivan.

"Well, I thank you, Mr. Sullivan. It has been a difficult year," replied the president.

"This is a beautiful office," remarked Sullivan.

"Yes, it is," answered the president, "and we have a beautiful garden. Would you like to see it?"

Sullivan nodded yes, and an assistant came out of nowhere to open the glass doors to the garden. The president and Sullivan walked into the rose garden, and we followed.

"Do you have a garden, Mr. Sullivan?" the president asked.

"Oh, no," answered Sullivan. "Sylvia and I live in an apartment in New York City. I love living in the city. And I walk everywhere."

"When I come to New York City, I would enjoy seeing one of your shows," said the president.

"It would be my pleasure," replied Sullivan, and turning to me said, "Bernie, be sure to keep in touch with President Johnson's people."

"I am sorry you didn't get a chance to meet Mrs. Johnson, but perhaps we all can get together on your next trip to Washington," offered the president. Just then an aide signaled to the president that they had to move along.

"You'll have to excuse me," suggested the president. "I have a late meeting scheduled with the vice president." He quickly shook each person's hand and left the room, followed by the assistant and the photographers.

The entire meeting took less than ten minutes, but Sullivan was thrilled with it.

His only remark to me as we left was, "I thought he looked a little tired."

9
When Ed Sullivan Broke
Television's "Color Line"

Many people may be aware that Ed Sullivan was "color blind" when it came to booking talent for his television series. At the outset of his career as a sports reporter, Sullivan was color blind from the start, writing about African-American sports stars with his very first job on the *Port Chester Item*. Few realize, perhaps, that *The Ed Sullivan Show* was the first television program to integrate an African-American dancer into the show's permanent dancing chorus, breaking the "color line" in the medium for the first time.

Sullivan's family and friends were not surprised by the move, but it was all but ignored at the time when artists of color were still relegated to subservient roles in television and motion pictures. The civil rights issues were at their height during the late 1950s and '60s, but from the outset of his television series, Ed Sullivan had booked African-American stars on his variety show. His list of guest performers included Nat King Cole, Lena Horne, Diahann Carroll, Ethel Waters, Pearl Bailey, Lesley Uggams, Eartha Kitt, Bill Cosby, Flip Wilson, Johnny Mathis, the Temptations, the Four Tops, Dewey "Pigmeat" Markham, Moms Mabley, Sammy Davis Jr., the Supremes, Pegleg Bates, Ray Charles, James Brown, Duke Ellington, Count Basie, and, no doubt Sullivan's favorite jazz artist, Louis Armstrong.

It is little known that when Bill "Bojangles" Robinson died pen-

Ed enjoying a moment with two of his favorite performers, singer
Tony Bennett and jazz great Duke Ellington. (Sullivan Productions)

niless, Sullivan paid for his funeral and organized a funeral procession as a tribute to the great dancer. Sullivan invited dozens of stars
to participate in the "Bojangles" funeral procession, so on Bill Robinson's last trip through Harlem, he was accompanied by dozens
of stars of the entertainment world, including Danny Kaye, Tony
Bennett, Eartha Kitt, and Pearl Bailey. The procession started from
Harlem and advanced down Broadway to Times Square. It was reported that more than half a million people lined the streets to view
Mr. Bojangles's last trip down the Great White Way.

When it came to booking entertainers for his show, Sullivan was
quoted as saying that all he looks for is great talent and never the
color of skin. The fact that Sullivan frequently booked African-
American talent did not sit well with his sponsors. The executives
at Emerson Radio, his first sponsor, and later at Lincoln Mercury
were concerned that their dealerships in the South would not be

Sammy Davis Jr., who first appeared on *The Ed Sullivan Show* as the star of the Will Mastin Trio, made eight appearances on the show as a soloist. (Photofest)

pleased, and television audiences in Southern states would tune out. Sullivan proved them wrong in both cases. *The Ed Sullivan Show* always had top rating numbers in the South, Sullivan informed the sponsors, and to the dealership problem he said, "If they don't like it, then they can leave. No one is going to tell me how to book my show."

The integration of the permanent chorus line was not planned, but grew out of an incident in December 1961, in which the stars

Sullivan's special talent was anticipating the interest and curiosity of his audience. His training and career as a journalist made him aware of who the public wanted to see on his show, so it was not out of place for him to invite Coretta Scott King to appear on his stage after the murder of her husband, the civil rights leader Dr. Martin Luther King Jr. Mrs. King made an impassioned appeal for tolerance. (Photofest)

of the all-American football team were invited to appear on the show. In this segment, each football star was to be escorted onto the stage by a dancer who would "dance them to the center of the stage." Bobby Bell, from the University of Minnesota, was the only African-American football player in the group of all-stars, and Sullivan arranged for a talented African-American dancer, Myrna White, to bring him on stage.

Two days after the show, Sullivan received a call from an editor at *Jet* magazine who informed Sullivan that they had received more than one hundred phone calls and letters objecting to the racial pairing. Sullivan was surprised at the call, but made an instant decision to solve the problem. "If you want a real news story, here's one. Myrna White is becoming a member of our chorus line. It will be the first permanent integrated dancing chorus line in television. Now that's a scoop."

Jet magazine ran the story and it broke nationally in the television columns.

The move was a good example of Sullivan's instinctive ability to recognize a problem and solve it with great dispatch. He would have made an excellent public relations counselor had he chosen that line of work.

10
Topo Gigio and the Obratsov Puppets

E d Sullivan envisioned his role on the show as primarily an on-camera host and, more importantly, chief booker of talent. For many years his extraordinary ability to anticipate the interest of the television viewing audience was ignored by the critics and press. They insisted on just reviewing his role as the host of the show and were quick to point out his deficiencies in that department. On rare occasions, Sullivan would join a guest as a "straight man" for a comedy routine. He did this with Ricky Lane and Velvel, the oft-booked ventriloquist; with Soupy Sales in a comedy sketch; and occasionally with a singer in an impromptu duet—but there was one act in which Sullivan was cast as a partner. That was his little comic interludes with Topo Gigio, a ten-inch rubbery mouse-like puppet that appeared on the show fifty times.

Topo Gigio made its first appearance on the show on April 14, 1963. Sullivan had seen tape of Topo from a television program in Italy and booked the puppet for a series of appearances, without realizing that he would be part of the act. It became evident when the puppet group arrived (there were three puppeteers handling the puppet's movements and a fourth person as Topo's voice) that someone would be needed to feed lines to Topo Gigio. Sullivan stepped in for the initial appearance, planning to replace himself with a professional comic if Topo was a hit with the audience. It was evident from the very first appearance, however, that the chemistry between Sullivan and Topo Gigio worked extremely well. The exchanges between Sullivan and the mouse-like puppet revealed another side of the host, a warm and humanizing element that otherwise was rarely evident in the rigid, "poker-faced" host.

The team of three puppeteers controlled Topo Gigio with short sticks, much like the manner in which puppets in China and India are handled. The puppeteers were dressed all in black with black hoods and stood in front of a black velvet drape, which made them invisible to the television audience, as well as most of the people seated in the Ed Sullivan Theater. The creator of Topo Gigio, Maria Perego, controlled the movement of the mouth. Federico Gioli was the puppeteer who operated Topo's hands, while his wife, Anabella Gioli, moved the puppets large ears, which were reminiscent of the famed Disney mouse named Mickey.

The Topo Gigio act apparently worked so well because Sullivan had the ability to talk to the puppet as if it were a live little kid. He often said that when he did the routines with Topo, he felt as if he were talking to a real little boy, and he spoke of Topo in interviews with the same special reserve he had for children. I never saw him refuse an autograph to a "youngster," his favorite word for children. Sullivan was very aware that there were children in his audience. The show aired early enough to have a substantial number of children in his viewing audience. When introducing circus acts, Sullivan would often say, "And here is something special for the youngsters in the audience." (Incidentally, he was also very aware that his program was carried "live" throughout Canada, and so he would often add, "And the youngsters here and in Canada.")

The tagline to the routine with Topo Gigio was always Topo's request that Sullivan kiss him, or as Topo exclaimed, "Eddie, keees-a-me Goood Night." The line became famous and it was not unusual for passersby to call out, "Eddie, keees-a-me Goood Night" as Sullivan walked the streets of New York.

The Topo Gigio appearances probably softened Sullivan's stilted

Sullivan rarely appeared with one of his performers, but he made an exception in the case of Topo Gigio. Ed played "straight man" to Topo's comedy patter, making them the most unusual comedy team in television history. Topo Gigio made fifty appearances on *The Ed Sullivan Show*. (Photofest)

appearance as a host and were no doubt important in deepening the audience's feeling about Sullivan as a real person. It seems ironic that a puppet helped humanize Sullivan more than anything else he did on his show.

On Ed Sullivan's closing show, in 1971, Sullivan invited Topo Gigio to appear with him as the closing act, and again Topo requested, for the last time, "Eddie, keeees-a-me Goood Night."

To open his summer season in 1967, Ed Sullivan brought Frank Sinatra, Tony Bennett, and Topo Gigio. It was the first time this trio of some of Ed's favorite performers appeared on *The Ed Sullivan Show* together. Illustration by Texas artist Tom Crabtree. (Photofest)

Few remember that in addition to devoting an entire sixty-minute program to one dance group such as the Bolshoi Ballet or the Moiseyev Dancers, Sullivan also brought to his television audience other cultural entertainment such as the Obratsov Russian Puppet Theater. In the fall of 1963, Sol Hurok brought the Obratsov group to New York for a run at the Broadway Theater. Hurok invited Sullivan to see the show on opening night, and after viewing the unique production, Sullivan decided to devote an entire hour to the act. (This was long before Jim Henson and "The Muppets" had made their everlasting impression on *Sesame Street*.) Far from being merely an act for children, Sergei Obratsov's puppets were the foremost puppet group in Russia, and Obratsov had his own theater in Moscow.

Previewing the show in their November 30, 1963, issue, *TV Guide* gave it this "Close-Up":

> Tonight Ed reaches past the iron curtain for an entire hour with the Obratsov Russian Puppet Theater, presenting an "Unusual Concert."
>
> Satire is Obratsov's specialty. Every show needs an emcee, and this emcee is smooth indeed. He in turn introduces "The Coloratura Soprano"; "The Tango"; "The Wunderkind," a unique prodigy; "The Gypsies" from the forest of Trancaucasia; "The Performing Animals," terpsichorean poodles; "The Illusionist"; "The Tap Dancers"; "Jazz Singer and her Combo," an act so far out according to the official program that it's "a likely nominee for the first U.S.A.-USSR joint moon shot."
>
> Obratsov first came to the United States in 1925 as an actor with the Russian Art Theater. Tonight's 60 minute performance was taped last month at the conclusion of the troupe's Broadway engagement, a part of the American-Soviet cultural exchange.[1]

It is interesting to note that the Obratsov Russian Puppet Theater was considered cultural—and "high" culture at that—in Russia, and also by the American critics who viewed their performances at the Broadway Theater. It is also important to note that this booking of an outstanding Russian act took place during the height of the cold war. Although a few cultural exchanges took place between the United States and Russia, such as the Obratsov Puppets and the Bolshoi Ballet troupe, the Cuban missile crisis was still in the minds of many Americans, and the Berlin Wall stood as a constant reminder of the continuing state of tension between the two countries.

11
Sullivan Brings Opera and Classical Music to Television

Ed Sullivan was the first producer in television to bring live opera to a wide national television audience. As John Leonard notes in *A Really Big Show*, "In 1953, live from the stage of the Met, he [Sullivan] telecast part of the last act of *Carmen* with Risë Stevens and Richard Tucker, to approving reviews and audience acclaim. (So much for public television's higher-than-thoubrow patting itself on the back for having been the first to do such a thing twenty-four years later.)"[1]

In 1956, Ed Sullivan brought opera to television in a grand manner. He made an arrangement with Rudolf Bing, the managing director of the Metropolitan Opera Company, to feature five of the Met's opera productions on five Sunday nights and to pay the Met one hundred thousand dollars for the performances and television rights. At that time, one hundred thousand dollars was decidedly over Sullivan's budget; however, Sullivan was intent on bringing high cultural entertainment to his audience, along with his platoon of comedians and animal acts. Moreover, he promised Mr. Bing to give each opera segment at least eighteen minutes on each program. When you consider that most singers are given four or five minutes for their turn, eighteen minutes is an enormous chunk of the show, which ran fifty-two minutes (eight minutes were devoted to commercials and promotional announcements).

On November 26, 1956, the first opera was presented. It was a scene from *Tosca* and featured the television debut of Maria Callas, who later gained worldwide fame. The long opera segment was a critical success, but according to the Trendex report, not a winner in the race for ratings. It caused the show to drop six important rating points from its usual high numbers.

Undismayed, Sullivan tried again on January 27, 1957, with the second of the six commitments with the Met. Sullivan presented Dorothy Kirsten in *Madame Butterfly*, and again it was a disappointment. This time, Sullivan lost not only rating points, but the 8 p.m. to 9 p.m. time slot, which his show usually dominated. Sullivan came in third against ABC and NBC. Both Sullivan and Bing were unhappy with the results. On Sunday, March 10, 1957, Sullivan tried again with Metropolitan stars Renata Tebaldi and Richard Tucker singing a duet from *La Bohème*. But by then Sullivan had learned his lesson. This segment from the Met was cut to a four-minute spot. Mr. Bing was not happy with the arrangement, and so the contract to bring Metropolitan Opera productions to the Sullivan stage was discontinued. Nevertheless, it did not dim Sullivan's taste for presenting opera stars on his show. In fact, the frequency increased. In the 1960s, Sullivan featured an opera star, ballet dancer, or classical musician on almost every show, but eighteen-minute operas were not repeated. Sullivan had discovered that his audience would accept and enjoy these highbrow artists, but only in short takes.

Sullivan booked soprano Roberta Peters soon after her surprise triumph as a substitute for an ailing Metropolitan star in *Don Giovanni*. Ms. Peters was a hit. Sullivan called her "the little Cinderella from the Bronx" and brought the talented and beautiful singer back to his stage a total of forty-one times over the next years, more than any other classical or popular singer.

We can surmise why Ed Sullivan wanted to present opera on his show. Opera stars gave the show a patina of class, brought in a

Roberta Peters. (Photofest)

wider and upgraded audience, and gave the program an interesting mix of variety. John Leonard attempts to explain why opera singers and their managers were so anxious to have them appear on *The Ed Sullivan Show*: "What you may wonder, was in it for the Met or La Scala? After all they were permitted only snippets. . . . Well there was *money and publicity*, and opera stars are mostly hams, and Beverly Sills went on to direct the New York City Opera (and currently all of Lincoln Center), and Robert Merrill would get to sing the national anthem at every New York Yankees home game, and so Ed's show must have been a shrewd career move."[2]

Bernard Gurtman, a manager of classical artists, who I interviewed on the same topic, insisted that every manager of opera singers and classical musicians wanted to place their clients on the Sullivan show. He felt, as many others did, that it exposed these stars to a whole new audience, and that it increased their salaries and bookings in a way no other television show could match. "The publicity and promotion was invaluable to a classical artist," said Gurtman.[3]

Here is John Leonard's tongue-in-cheek appraisal of Ed Sullivan's ability to "read an audience":

It's also tempting to think of opera on the Sullivan Show as the first music video, except that Ed over the years hardened in his firm opinion that the American public preferred seeing the singers in evening clothes rather than costumes. Let's pause for a minute to consider this. Is it true? It must be, because Ed said so, and who else would know? He was as good at reviewing the public as, say Pauline Kael was at reviewing movies. It was Kael who told us that "when opera singers go into the movies, the baritones can act but the tenors can't."[4]

In an interview with Susan Elliott of the *New York Post* (February 12, 1988), Samuel Ramey, the Metropolitan Opera star baritone, recalled, "The first time I heard an opera singer was on *The Ed Sullivan Show.*"[5] Although the interview was devoted mainly to promoting Mr. Ramey's appearance on the Public Television series *Great Performances,* on which he sang the title role of Mozart's *Don Giovanni*, Ramey reflected upon how *The Ed Sullivan Show* opened his eyes to the world of opera.

In the interview, Ramey spoke about the importance of television to his career, and the career of other operatic performers. Ms. Elliott writes, "Born and raised in Colby, Kansas, Ramey appreciates television's value as a showcase for the performing arts. 'The first time I ever heard an opera singer was on *The Ed Sullivan Show.* I'd never been exposed to opera at all before then. I remember seeing Roberta Peters. I just fell madly in love with her.'"[6]

Ramey added, "Television has definitely had a positive effect, both for my career and for performing arts in general." Television also allowed him to connect to others in other meaningful ways: "My mother lives in the middle of Kansas. Since she's too old to travel now, TV is the only way she gets to see her son perform."[7]

In May 1996, I interviewed Robert Merrill about his many appearances on *The Ed Sullivan Show* beginning in 1949, before the program had a national hook-up. Merrill, who was born Merrill Miller and later changed his name to make it more theatrical, began his career as an entertainer in the Catskill Mountains at resort hotels like Grossinger's, Kutsher's, the Nevele, and Tamarack Lodge. He was only a teenager, but big for his age, and his handsome looks and booming voice brought him to the attention of agents and managers. Merrill's first agent was Moe Gale, head of the Associated Booking Agency. Gale, who specialized in booking his clients into nightclubs and theaters, also represented some of the finest jazz stars such as Louis Armstrong, Count Basie, and Ella Fitzgerald, but he let all of his associates know that Robert Merrill was one of his favorites because, "He not only has a great voice; he has class."

Merrill recalled, "I was paid $250 for my first appearance on the [Sullivan] show, and it took place about the time I began to make a mark with the Metropolitan Opera Company. I wasn't concerned about the money because I felt that it would help my career in opera, and for other personal appearances."[8]

Merrill went on to appear on the Sullivan show seventeen times, and his salary for each show rose to $2,500 when the Sullivan show was put on the full, national CBS Television Network. One of his appearances was televised live from the stage of the old Metropolitan Opera House as part of the deal Sullivan made with Rudolf Bing. Robert Merrill lauds Ed Sullivan for being "very brave in booking classical stars for his show, which really catered to a popular audience, and a large one at that."

Merrill continued,

I think Sullivan had good taste. Not because he booked me, but he put on the very best opera singers of our time: [Maria] Callas, Joan Sutherland, Roberta Peters, [Jan] Peerce, [Richard] Tucker, and other great performers. I remember he asked me to do a duet with

Robert Merrill. (Photofest)

Birgit Nilsson, one we had done at the Met. During the afternoon show, he had trouble pronouncing her first name, so I wrote it out phonetically for him, and he seemed to get it right, but when it came to the live show, at eight o'clock that night, Ed introduced us as, "From the Metropolitan Opera Company, here is Robert Merrill and *Bridget* Nilsson."

Merrill said that he thought that Sullivan was a master at "mixing up" the classical and popular artists. "Did you know that he booked me to appear on the same show as Elvis Presley? Now that's what I call reaching for a wide audience.

"I know that I had an easier time performing on the Sullivan show than most opera singers, because I started my career playing at popular theaters such as the Roxy [Theatre] and the Radio City Music Hall. I was at ease before a live audience, and had a quite a bit of experience before I entered the opera field."

As a rule, Rudolf Bing frowned upon having his Metropolitan Opera stars appear on the vaudeville stage or in Las Vegas night-clubs, as Robert Merrill often did, but Merrill was so popular. And, of course, Merrill's popularity was enhanced by his many appearances on the Sullivan show. According to Jim Murtha, Sol Hurok's press representative, there was little Rudolf Bing could do to contain this star.

Murtha was on Hurok's press relations staff during the 1950s and '60s, but left to form his own management and public relations agency with Bernard Gurtman, specializing in classical artists.[9] During that time, Gurtman and Murtha had a good deal of contact with *The Ed Sullivan Show* relating to the many classical artists, including Roberta Peters, Robert Merrill, Jan Peerce, Andrés Segovia, Isaac Stern, Itzhak Perlman, the Moiseyev Dancers, and many others.

I interviewed Bernard Gurtman in 1997 and again in 2006. When asked about how the managers of classical artists viewed the Sullivan show, Gurtman indicated that it was tremendously important. "The beauty of the Sullivan Show was the 'variety mix.' Sullivan would have a classical artist along with [comic] Myron Cohen and an elephant act. It was the 'mix' that worked. He mixed the classical with the clowning to give the show enough variety to hold the audience. If you didn't like something, you just waited, and in the next three minutes there would be something you might like better."

According to Gurtman, "those three-minute turns" on the Sullivan show meant a lot to all kinds of performers. "It probably couldn't be done today. Take a classical artist like [pianist/conductor] Peter Nero, or even someone like [comic] Alan King might not make it without those three-minute spots."

Gurtman compared opera singers to baseball players:

Being with the Metropolitan Opera was like being with the New York Yankees. You had to be a *team player*. The Yankees didn't feature any particular star. The Metropolitan Opera directors didn't want a Robert Merrill or a Roberta Peters to stand out from the company, but *The Ed Sullivan Show* gave them the opportunity to do just that. Rather than dressed in costume, Merrill would appear on the Sullivan show in a tux or a business suit. Merrill became a recognizable face. The publicity surrounding his appearance on the Sullivan show increased his value as a concert artist, and that is where the big payoff in fame and monetary rewards occurs in the classical field.

Gurtman continued,

The real money and rewards are in the recitals. When you went out on "the road," to perform concerts in cities all over America, you had to sell tickets. Appearances on *The Ed Sullivan Show* helped to sell those tickets. In an opera you were a faceless singer. You were in costume. You could not stand out. However, on the Sullivan show, the audience saw you as a real person. You stood out from the crowd. In those three minutes, the audience had a chance to see you as an individual, not a team player. Here you were in street clothes doing the most popular arias. Even Callas, Roberta Peters, Anna Moffo . . . they came on not in opera clothes, but in gowns and tailored clothes. Moreover, these great divas were shown in tight close-ups, so the television audience could really see what they looked like. The appearances on the Sullivan show projected these artists to a broader public, made them human, and created an interest in people who may have never seen an opera. It nurtured and built up a concert hall audience in this country for these classical artists, who could go out and perform a full concert or recital and earn more money (and personal acclaim). I think that was one of the great virtues of the Sullivan show, that Sullivan never got credit for.

The Ed Sullivan Show helped create a national audience for classical musicians, singers, and dancers, a television platform that is not available today. In their three minutes on the Sullivan show, classical artists were given a chance to be seen by the general public who never attended a concert or an opera performance. In Sullivan's audience there might be a mechanic from Pittsburgh or a farmer in Kansas or a Macy's salesperson, who would never go to a classical recital to see these artists in a concert hall setting, because it would be considered to be "high class" or "artsy." Sullivan always presented the opera singers and the ballet dancers with the attitude that these were "class" performers. He respected their talent, and the audience accepted them on that level.

As Gurtman observed,

Whether it was intentional on the part of Sullivan or Bob Precht to present all of these classical attractions, we don't know. How much was conscious, how much was calculated, how much was unconscious, we may never know. It might have been Sullivan's way of creating variety the way he created it in his [newspaper] column where he wrote items about the high[brow] and low[brow]. The column [Toast of the Town] was all over the lot. You could read Sullivan's column the way he did his show. It covered everything. That's why it was so valuable to be on the Sullivan show all the time for the artists. It was an outlet to the world. And it was the new medium in the late fifties. In 1962, I believe, it began to be telecast in color so it was a great exposure. It was different from Firestone [*The Voice of Firestone* television show] and some of the other television shows. One of the Firestone programs, hosted by Don Vorhees, was strictly devoted to classical music, but it drew a much smaller television audience than the Sullivan show. . . .

You don't have that kind of thing today and that's why I'm into more pop things. [His most prominent client for the last twenty years was the comedian/pianist Victor Borge, who died in 2005.] The promotion of classical artists to the masses is gone, and you are not educating the future generations [to classical music and artists].

Gurtman reiterated that he believed that *The Ed Sullivan Show* "educated" the mass public to classical music and its artists, along with Leonard Bernstein's "Young People's Concerts" on Saturday mornings. "But all those shows are gone today."

Gurtman noted that public television fills in the gap to a certain select audience, but pointed out that there is no regular PBS series devoted to classical music. However, to fill the concert halls, it is still necessary to popularize the classical scene. He said that a current example is Pavarotti and the Three Tenors concerts, which take place in stadiums with capacities in the tens of thousands.

"People will go to Giants Stadium or Yankee Stadium and pay fifty or a hundred dollars to see these attractions," said Gurtman. The Three Tenors, and now the Three Sopranos, were seen on PBS Television specials, which brought them to the attention of the general public, much in the way the Sullivan show did. The Three Sopranos were relatively unknown opera singers, but the fact that they were packaged similarly to the Three Tenors led to their success.

Gurtman also said that in the early part of the century, the immigrants to this country had a heritage of culture. Even though they were poor, many of the immigrants heard classical music in their homes, especially if they were from Italy, France, and Germany.

With the second and third generations of these immigrants in America, this musical heritage began to fade.

"I always believed that classical music was like good scotch," Gurtman asserted.

> You have to develop a taste for classical music. And how can you develop this acquired taste, when you can't afford to go to the opera and pay one hundred dollars for a ticket? During the sixties and the seventies there were other variety television shows that presented classical musicians and singers, but the producers of these other shows often treated classical performers in a comedic way or poked fun at. On the other hand, Sullivan introduced the classical artists as if they were important. The singers on the Sullivan show would sing a little aria, or half an aria as the case may be, and it was presented as an important, and even serious spot. This approach stretched and educated the audience to "serious music."

Gurtman remembered that Sullivan had the Moiseyev Dancers on his show in 1958, when the troupe came to New York City to perform at the old Metropolitan Opera House. It was important to appear on *The Ed Sullivan Show* to promote their American tour. He said that today you would have to play *The Tonight Show* twenty times before you could make the kind of impact that was made with one shot on the Sullivan show.

> The Met was not happy about Merrill's television appearances, and [was] even less happy about Merrill's appearances in Las Vegas. I think he appeared in Las Vegas with Louis Armstrong. In fact, I think he did a sketch where he traded places with Armstrong, and Louis came out as the classical singer and Bob entered as the jazz singer. And Merrill appeared in a movie, *Aaron Slick from Punkin Crick*. Rudolf Bing was not happy to see his Met stars appear in Las

Vegas or in a popular film, but Robert Merrill was at the height of his popularity, and he could do that kind of thing.

Gurtman also pointed out that Merrill came out of the popular field and had his own NBC radio show before he came to the Met. He was a popular personality, and the Met could not contain him as they could their other performers. But the Sullivan show, according to Merrill, was probably most important in bringing the mass audiences to his recitals.

Gurtman added that the Sullivan show helped not only to build an audience for classical recitals, but to sell classical records as well.

Artists and managers understood that appearing on the Sullivan show was important to their careers. Sullivan always presented the artist in a favorable light. He never demeaned a performer. He didn't ask them to appear in skits, as in other variety shows. On *The Danny Kaye Show* and *The Milton Berle Show*, for instance, you could sing for a few minutes, but then you had to be in the sketches. You couldn't just go on the show and be "you."

The impact on this new audience for classical performers was enormous. For instance take the Moiseyev and the Bolshoi. They appeared here when we were still engaged in the "cold war." Sullivan took Russian attractions, not that long after McCarthyism, and put them on national television. That's amazing. It is still amazing to me. It took the wall down and presented them as international artists allowing them to have stature, and not reducing them to a "cold war" enemy and all the other things that went on at that time. And it was fantastic for their tour here. You couldn't buy that type of advertising.

Some of the artists Sol Hurok put on the show included Itzhak Perlman, Isaac Stern, the great Spanish classical guitarist Segovia, and opera singer Marian Anderson. Gurtman recalled that Roberta

Peters, Jan Peerce, and Robert Merrill were other Hurok artists who appeared on the Sullivan show many times.

Gurtman formed his own management/PR company with Jim Murtha, and one of their early clients was Placido Domingo. Although Domingo was not yet well-known, his ego was considerable. Murtha and Gurtman felt that an appearance on *The Tonight Show Starring Johnny Carson* would be a good springboard for Domingo's career. After *The Ed Sullivan Show* had been off television for several years, Sullivan's formula for presenting entertainment was still implemented. Gurtman took Domingo out to Los Angeles for an audition for the Carson show. Fearing that Domingo, with his ego, might turn down an audition, the singer was told it was a booking. Fortunately, Domingo's audition, which Gurtman called a "rehearsal," worked out well, and the producers of *The Tonight Show* quickly recognized that Domingo's singing talent *and* charisma were overwhelming. Domingo appeared often on the Carson show, which was one of the few network shows to occasionally feature a classical artist, following the pattern Sullivan had set.

More than two decades after its last program, *The Ed Sullivan Show* spawned an unusual videocassette. In 1994, Bernard Gurtman realized that there were virtually no filmed performances of many famous stars of the 1950s and '60s—at least, not in close-up, and not performing their most popular arias. He remembered that he had arranged for the appearances of many of these famous opera singers on *The Ed Sullivan Show* and decided to track down the video recordings of those performances.

Gurtman discovered that the Sullivan archives were controlled by Andrew Solt, who had purchased them from Sullivan Productions for his SOFA Productions. In fact, SOFA is the only company that has a treasure trove of videotaped performances of the Beatles, Elvis Presley, and the Rolling Stones on *The Ed Sullivan Show*, as well as appearances of Maria Callas, Joan Sutherland, and scores of other world-famous classical artists. Gurtman met with Solt and they worked out a financial arrangement, which made the opera videocassette a reality. Gurtman and his music editors spent hundreds of hours viewing the Sullivan show performances of the opera stars and finally assembled a videocassette of nineteen outstanding appearances. Titled *Great Moments in Opera*, the collection features Richard Tucker singing "Vesti il guiba" from *Il Pagliacci*; Jan Peerce and Robert Merrill performing "Dueto final" from *La Forza Del Destino*; Joan Sutherland singing "Sempre libre" from *La Traviata*; Maria Callas's superb rendition of "Vissi d'arte" from *Tosca*; Roberta Peters singing "Una vocoe poco fa" from *Barber of Seville*; and additional rare performances by Leontyne Price, Beverly Sills, Marilyn Horne, Birgit Nilsson, Anna Moffo, Franco Corelli, Eileen Farrell, Dorothy Kirsten, Lily Pons, Renata Tebaldi, and others.

The collection is quite unique, because all the performances were live. As almost everything on television today is taped or recorded digitally, it may be difficult to imagine that *The Ed Sullivan Show* was always live. Sullivan felt that having the entertainers perform live in front of a real audience gave an edge to the whole show. Sullivan believed that the opera singers were more inclined to give their best performances in front of an audience that would respond to them as if they were performing in an opera or a concert hall. The nervous energy, Sullivan felt, added an element to the television show that could not be duplicated in filming or taping the performance.

12

Ed Speaks Out at the Fifteenth Anniversary of His Show

When *The Ed Sullivan Show* was nearing its fifteenth anniversary on the air, the CBS Press Department asked Sullivan to write an article for a special press book they were preparing to celebrate the occasion. It was to be distributed to television and media columnists and editors across the country. Sullivan was delighted to write the article, titled "Where Do We Go from Here?"

As we start our 16th year in television, after a continuous skein of 776 Sunday-night shows, a reasonable question is: "Where Do We Go from Here?" The inquiry is fair because from 1948 to 1963 our cameras were inside the Kremlin walls, we've played to an audience of befurred Eskimos in Kotzebue, Alaska, we've entertained 250,000 Russians in Moscow and Leningrad, we've done our show from the decks of battleships and carriers, we've played to U.S. troops in Guantanamo and Berlin, and from the bridge of refugees outside Hong Kong we've brought you footage on the patrols of Red China guards. From Asia, Europe, South America and from our own country, Sunday and Sunday we have entertained you with great stars of ballet, opera, puppetry, circuses—singers, dancers, novelty acts, movie stars.

Well let's look at the record of the past 15 years and try to make a forecast of things to come. We can agree, to start with, that there are certain television firsts which we cannot create in years to come.

Never again, for instance, can we bring you the television debut of Walt Disney as we did on February 8, 1953. We introduced him to your homes in an unforgettable full-hour show, highlighted by his historic re-creation of the actual writing of "Who's Afraid of the Big Bad Wolf?"

Never again can we bring you Grace Kelly, now the Princess of Monaco, singing and dancing on our stage with Ralph Meeker on that delightful French lesson from *Good News*.

Never again can we present, in their television debuts on our stage, the team of Martin and Lewis. That happened on our very first show in 1948, and on the same program two giants also made their television debuts—Richard Rodgers and the late Oscar Hammerstein II. Moments like these simply can't happen again— certainly not with the original cast!

Back in 1950 we started using excerpts from Broadway shows. On October 8, 1950, Ethel Waters, Julie Harris and Brandon de Wilde contributed a magnificent scene from *Member of the Wedding*. A few months later David Niven thrilled our audience in a scene from *Journey's End*. This was followed by Yul Brynner's brilliant "A Puzzlement" from *The King and I* and the late Gertrude Lawrence singing "I Whistle a Happy Tune." Helen Hayes did an excerpt from *Victoria Regina* and *The Wisteria Trees*, and Martha Scott won applause in *Coquette*.

The great Alfred Lunt was magnificent in Robert E. Sherwood's *There Shall Be No Night*.

Fredric March recalled *The Best Years of Our Lives*; James Mason and his wife Pamela did a scene from *The Road to Rome*; a youthful Barbara Bel Geddes teamed with a young Barry Nelson in *Waterloo Bridge* and Audrey Hepburn made her television bow on our stage with a brilliant portrayal in *Nine Days a Queen*. We saved *All the Way Home* by presenting Arthur Hill in a gripping scene; box office disaster became a roaring success!

Back in 1952 we brought America the first national experience with the glittering prose of Christopher Fry. This was Fry's magnificent *Venus Observed*, in which Rex Harrison and Lilli Palmer

Bert Lahr, known by most people for his role as the Cowardly Lion in the classic film *The Wizard of Oz*, was a favorite of Ed Sullivan's. Lahr appeared on the show seventeen times. (Photofest)

were superb. A few months later Harrison joined Audrey Hepburn in our theatre for *Anne of a Thousand Days*. Then Henry Fonda won national plaudits for our show as *Mister Roberts*, along with James Cagney and Jack Lemmon in other scenes from that great hit.

Gary Cooper and Rod Steiger brought our audience to its feet, cheering, in an unforgettable trial scene from *The Court-Martial of Billy Mitchell*. Robert Mitchum and Shelly Winters won bravos in *Night of the Hunter*, and Noël Coward, backed by conductor Andre Kostelanetz and the New York Philharmonic, delighted the nation by interpreting Ogden Nash's witty treatment of Saint-Saëns' "Carnival of Animals." In ballet, as long ago as 1951, we introduced England's great ballerinas Margot Fonteyn and Moira Shearer in television-debut excerpts from *Sleeping Beauty* and *Swan Lake*. We introduced to this country and Canada, Russia's brilliant Moiseyev Ballet and Japan's graceful Takarazuka girl dancers. Our stage has been graced by Nora Kaye, John Gilpin, Carmen Lavallade and Russia's Maya Plisetskaya. Miss Kaye danced with Scott Douglas on our show from Portugal and went with us to Moscow and Leningrad. We had exciting excerpts from Jerome Robbins' "Ballets: USA" and a ballet by Robert Butler when we did our show from Spoleto, Italy.

In the field of grand opera we have not only originated our program from the stage of New York's Metropolitan Opera House but down the years we featured nearly every great opera star.

On the night that Maria Callas made her television debut in 1956 she did a segment from "Tosca" with George London. Instead of using a staff conductor, we engaged the late Dimitri Mitropolous to conduct the Metropolitan Opera Orchestra. As the narrator we were fortunate to have Rudolph Bing. Miss Callas has been described as temperamental, but I never met a more charming person in the entire 15 years of our show.

Australia's Joan Sutherland has thrilled our audience. Roberta Peters' maiden television outing was before our cameras, the first of her 34 appearances with us. Eileen Farrell, Leontyne Price, Risë Stevens, Robert Merrill, Cesare Siepi, Jan Peerce, Jerome Hines are only part of an endless parade of opera stars we have featured.

In July, 1956, when every youngster in our country was downcast at the closing of the Ringling Brothers Circus, in Pittsburgh, we rushed all of the stars of the show to our theater and gave the country a solid hour of circus thrills. Part of this was done on our stage, but acts like the ill-fated Wallendas and the startling cannon act of the Zacchinis performed outdoors, a half-block from the studio. The only thing that we couldn't give to the country and Canada that thrilling Sunday night was pink lemonade.

This illustration by Tom Crabtree highlights the breadth and variety of guests
Ed featured nearly every Sunday night during the program's lengthy run. (Photofest)

The tragedy that later befell the Wallendas was a personal shock because I knew them so well. I wish that American circuses would insist that aerial acts work above a protective net that could catch them, in case of a single misstep. In Europe aerial acts work with a safety wire attached to their bodies, and European audiences don't seem to miss a thrill.

So you can well ask, and we can well wonder, where do we go from here?

Never again can we present the television debuts of Cole Porter or producer Joshua Logan, or the electronic bow of a gifted trio—

Alan Jay Lerner, Frederick Loewe and the late Moss Hart—as we did on March 3, 1957, with our presentation of their *My Fair Lady*, starring the lovely Julie Andrews, Stanley Holloway, Edward Mulhare, Michael King, Rodney McLennnon, Gene Kelly, Leslie Caron, Fred Astaire and Jane Powell.

It would be impossible to unite Richard Burton, Miss Andrews and Robert Goulet for the first television viewing of *Camelot*. That was in March of 1961, and today Burton and Goulet are two of the greatest matinee idols in show business.

We can't re-create the initial television appearances on our stage of Dean Martin and Jerry Lewis, Lena Horne, Bob Hope, Dinah Shore, Eddie Fisher and the late Charles Laughton. These were all great moments and part of television history.

For his appearance with us on May 8, 1949, I asked Laughton if he would like to do a Bible reading. I presented one condition: that Laughton, with his vast film background and brilliant stagecraft, direct the scene himself. This was a tremendous tour de force. In a nearby restaurant a youngster heard the Laughton reading and rushed over to the studio, then the Maxine Elliott Theater on West 39th Street. The youngster told Laughton that he would like to present him in a national tour of Bible readings. Laughton agreed. The youngster was Paul Gregory, and the success of this led later to the Gregory-Laughton productions of *Don Juan in Hell*, *John Brown's Body* and other magnificent things in which Laughton, Charles Boyer and the late Tyrone Power participated.

Where do we go from here? Where can we find anyone to match the readings of Carl Sandburg, Anthony Quinn and Charles Laughton? Where can we find a concert pianist to exceed Van Cliburn, Eugene List and Grant Johanssen? Where can we find another Louis "Satchmo" Armstrong? Where can we find material to match the drama of the Cole Porter story, the Richard Rodgers story, the Josh Logan story, the Robert E. Sherwood story, the Oscar Hammerstein story and the Helen Hayes story? Where can we get a young recording star to match the excitement created by Elvis Presley on our stage?

Are there upcoming singers who will match Connie Francis, Brenda Lee, Ann-Margret, Paul Anka, Eddie Fisher, Frankie Avalon, Fabian and Johnny Mathis? Will there be, in the near future, great singers of the caliber of Kate Smith, Ella Fitzgerald, Peggy Lee and Patti Page? Is there an accordion player to compare to Dick Contino, who astounded the 250,000 Russians we entertained on our trip to that country?

What shows of the 15 years do I best remember? The night in

More often than any other network program, *The Ed Sullivan Show* brought the stars of the jazz world to an audience of millions. Jazz legend Ella Fitzgerald was a frequent guest. (Photofest)

1958 when Maurice Chevalier and Sophie Tucker tore the house down with their moving duet of "I Remember It Well" is one. Here were two great veteran stars at the very peak of their artistry. Similarly, any night that Jimmy Durante has been on our stage with Sonny King and Eddie Jackson has been an unforgettable experience. And when Durante, after 20 minutes of comedy, sits at the piano and sings "Young at Heart," he touches the heart of every adult in the audience.

Another never-to-be-forgotten night: when Bing Crosby, Phil Silvers and Julie Andrews engaged in a magnificent underplayed comedy. I'll never forget, either, Burt Lancaster and Tony Curtis in our theatre, Burt doing some of the starting acrobatic tricks he once did in the circus. Lancaster had to go into strict training for almost a month to condition himself for this. But you can measure the greatness of a performer by the sacrifices he makes to prepare himself for an appearance.

When you speak of comics, you can't forget the comedian who never has lost his respect for an audience. That is Jack Carter, and our recent visit to Toronto's magnificent O'Keefe Center Theatre Carter, or rather the tumultuous applause of the audience for Carter, stopped the show. He is a true clown, this Carter. He thinks amusingly. Similarly, talented and equally conscientious is the Canadian comedy duo of Wayne and Shuster. They have made 43 appearances on our show, and they have never failed to score a smashing success. As another measure of distinction, Wayne and Shuster write their own material, as does the brilliant team of Rowan and Martin.

Will there ever be another singing combination to equal the McGuire Sisters or the Korean Kim Sisters? Who ever again will dance like Fred Astaire or clown with the brilliance of Lucille Ball? Or match the tones of Jane Powell, Ann Blyth, Dinah Shore or the wistfulness of Gertie Lawrence.

Our problem, after 15 years, is nothing new in the annals of show business. P. T. Barnum, Florenz Ziegfeld, the Shuberts, the

Ringlings, Sol Hurok, Billy Rose, George M. Cohan and other producers faced the same "where do we go from here" problem that confronts us now. The history of world show business proves there are always successors to the greats of today and the greats of yesterday. Youngsters come along and eventually fit the boots of their famous predecessors. We have seen this happen in the passage of a decade and a half because it happens every 24 hours.

I'll tell you why the stage-struck youngsters in 1963 have tremendous advantage over the stage-struck youngsters of years ago.

Today a kid with a natural knack for show business can sit at home and study, on his television set, the greatest performers in every field. Youngsters can analyze the techniques of great singers, great dancers, great actors, great comedians, great acrobats. And they can view them in close-up, to learn what they do—and most important—what NOT to do.

In the old days stage-struck youngsters had no such golden op portunities. I remember that famed actress Eva La Gallienne, recalling, in her book, the thrilling moment in Paris when her mother took her to see the great Sarah Bernhardt. Miss La Gallienne noted wistfully that because of the price of tickets, and their scarcity, her mother had to get two seats in one of the top galleries of the theater. She could hear the Divine Sarah's voice but could not see her facial expressions or the movements of her expressive hands.

Notwithstanding these difficulties, the Eva La Galliennes persisted in their ambitions and became stars in their own right. In 1963, with the television set in the living room serving as a continuous classroom blackboard, today's stage-struck kids can learn so very much about the techniques and skills of the theatre.

What change will there be in our particular type of electronic entertainment? Not very much, honestly. We have stepped up the pace and speed of our show down the years, eliminating everything that delays the presentation of the next act.

But the show-biz basics remain the same in drama, comedy and music—and YOU, the audience remain the same. You laugh at the same things, you are moved by the same things that touch the emotions, you thrill to the same brilliant instrumental or vocal passages in music. And you are just as appreciative as were your fathers and mothers. For instance, when we presented the Italian puppet show, the Piccoli Theatre, we had a mail response of over 13,000 letters. Thanks to all of you, Barnum nor Ziegfeld ever equaled that.

I promise you that we enter this 16th year of television with the same enthusiasm that marked our debut in 1948. I said then that I would never permit cheapness on our show and would never project into your living rooms something that I wouldn't permit the young members of my own family to see or hear.

I make this same pledge now and couple it with my sincere appreciation to all of you who have made our show the longest-lived in television.[1]

From this essay it is obvious Sullivan was proud of the quality of the performers he sought to present and the high level of their performances. He had an extraordinary sense of what the public would accept and even tested it by running the entire show in a dress rehearsal, a nonstop performance in front of a live audience of seven hundred people every Sunday from 1:00 p.m. to 2:00 p.m. The rehearsal show audience helped him prune and cull acts and material that did not go over well with this rehearsal audience. This testing method may well be the reason that *The Ed Sullivan Show* succeeded for twenty-four years.

Part II

Insights and Observations

Ed in the center surrounded by, clockwise from the top left, Sullivan and Topo Gigio, the Rolling Stones (Bill Wyman, Brian Jones, Mick Jagger, Charlie Watts, Keith Richards), Louis Armstrong, Red Skelton, Carol Burnett, Judy Garland, Art Garfunkel and Paul Simon, Ed and Elvis Presley, Ed with the Beatles (Ringo Starr, George Harrison, John Lennon, Paul McCartney). (Photofest)

13
Marlo Lewis, First Producer of
The Ed Sullivan Show,
Reveals Its Growing Pains

Marlo Lewis was the producer of *The Ed Sullivan Show* from its inception in 1948 until 1960. In the 1940s, Lewis was head of a small advertising firm, the Blaine-Thompson Agency, which specialized in theatrical advertising, particularly servicing clients associated with the Broadway scene. I spoke to Mr. Lewis on the phone in the late 1980s. He met Ed Sullivan when Ed was president of the New York Heart Fund. Upon his first meeting with the future showman, Lewis recalled, "Sullivan was different [from Walter Winchell, another columnist]. We saw that from the minute he [Sullivan] walked into our office. He wore no hat [Winchell always wore a fedora], he came alone, his voice was low and unobtrusive, he looked and dressed like a conservative businessman, and there wasn't a rumpled spot on him. Moreover, he had the time and taste for amenities; he thanked us for the meeting, expressed interest in our work. . . . Before long, and without too many second thoughts, we found ourselves deep into a discussion of the ways and means of planning the Heart Fund campaign."[1]

Lewis noted that Sullivan was a star-struck person: "Sullivan had a strong desire to be part of the entertainment world, that from the beginning of his newspaper career, his weekly schedule was filled with one personal appearance after another."[2]

Among the benefit performances Ed Sullivan organized were shows for Halloran Hospital in New York City, which attended to hospitalized servicemen during World War II and after. Sullivan drove to Philadelphia to present Victor Borge, ventriloquist Señor Wences, and singer Patti Page at a benefit gala for the Poor Richard Society. He traveled to Boston to organize a benefit for the Maris nuns. He was involved with numerous benefits for Catholic Charities and the B'Nai Brith, a Jewish charity organization. He even took a show, consisting of Vic Damone, comic Jackie Miles, and the legendary Sophie Tucker, to the Catskills for the birthday of Jennie Grossinger, the hostess of the famous Borscht Belt hotel that bears her family name. But it was Sullivan's yearly job as the master of ceremonies of the Harvest Moon Ball finals at Madison Square Garden that led, almost directly, to his career as the host of *The Ed Sullivan Show.*

Lewis said,

Cashing in on the popularity of ballroom dancing, the success of the Harvest Moon Ball, and the enormous promotion his newspaper [the *New York Daily News*] gave the event, Ed Sullivan found a way to insert himself into the ranks of headline performers. He signed up the winners, packaged them along with a few professional acts [singer Monica Lewis and ventriloquist Paul Winchell], gave himself the role of M.C., and using his clout as a gossip columnist, persuaded MGM to buy the whole kit and kaboodle for their Broadway movie theater, Loew's State. In the fall of 1947, the marquee of that theater read: ED SULLIVAN AND THE HARVEST MOON BALL WINNERS. Ed's name was up in lights. He was starring on Broadway.[3]

In his book, *Prime Time*, Marlo Lewis presents a different version of how Ed Sullivan was selected to be the host of his own variety program. In most references to *Toast of the Town*, as the show was originally called, Worthington Miner, a program executive at the Columbia Broadcasting System, is given credit for selecting Ed Sullivan to host the variety show. In Marlo Lewis's version, it was he who was instrumental in Sullivan becoming the series' master of ceremonies. According to Lewis, Sullivan was anxious to get into television, and he asked Marlo to contact the executives at CBS to see if they would be interested in having him host a program. At that time, Sullivan was writing his gossip column for the *New York Daily News*, the newspaper with the largest daily circulation in America, over a million copies daily. His column was also being distributed by the *New York Daily News*/*Chicago Tribune* Syndicate to more than two hundred newspapers across the country. He had personal contacts with most of the major entertainment and sports personalities of the day, and he was an experienced master of ceremonies of hundreds of benefit shows and professional vaudeville appearances. Sullivan had also been involved in a short-lived radio interview program in New York, the highpoint of which was introducing comedian Jack Benny to the radio medium for the first time.

According to Lewis, he called Jerry Danzig, a CBS executive, and presented the proposal to him, calling it Ed and Marlo's idea. Danzig seemed to like the idea but suggested that Marlo talk to Charles Underhill, Danzig's boss, and the head of programming for CBS. Marlo met with Underhill, who, without questioning the format of the show, asked him how soon he could put the show on.

It seemed that CBS was concerned about a variety show being planned by its rival, NBC. It had already moved to the planning stage and was to star the comedian Milton Berle. After his meeting with Underhill, Lewis received a phone call from a gentleman named Bill Gillette, who informed Marlo that he was the CBS liaison. Gillette asked Lewis to meet him at Sardi's, the popular show business restaurant. Knowing that the television business was often filled with intrigue, Lewis was not surprised when Gillette informed him that Underhill and Danzig were on their way "out." He said that William Paley, the chairman of CBS, was going to replace them with Tony (Worthington) Miner, who had a reputation as a strong producer of television drama but had little experience with variety or musical programs. Gillette assured Marlo Lewis that their variety show was still on safe ground because Tony Miner liked the idea of Sullivan hosting such a program. It seems Miner had caught Ed's performance at the Harvest Moon Ball finals and had been properly impressed by Sullivan.

When *Toast of the Town* finally premiered on June 20, 1948, Bill Gillette was in the control booth as its first director. His position was short-lived, though, because of his inexperience, which soon surfaced at rehearsals when he stormed out of the booth shouting at performers. He was replaced by John Wray, who directed the show for many years.

Since Marlo Lewis died several years ago, it is difficult to confirm exactly how much he had to do with the birth of the series, but there is no doubt that he did have a strong influence helping Sullivan shape the program in its early years. In his book, Marlo explains why Ed Sullivan often referred to Tony Miner as his "discoverer": After they closed the agreement with CBS, Lewis explained:

[I] brought Tony Miner to Ed's dressing room at the Roxy Theatre, where that year (1948) Ed and the Harvest Moon Ball winners were headlining the stage show. It was an interesting meeting. Miner delivered an extravagant paean in praise of Sullivan's performance as master of ceremonies of the Harvest Moon Ball in Madison Square Garden. He was eloquent, almost reverential in his admiration. Ed was overwhelmed. Miner's all-out tribute was unction to his soul, and forever after, Ed spoke and wrote of him with deep respect and gratitude. As the years passed, he even referred to Tony as the man who "discovered" him, the visionary who foresaw Ed's potentially great role in the fledgling television industry.[4]

14

Bob Precht, Producer of
The Ed Sullivan Show, Comments on
the Show and Its Cultural Aspects

In November 1996, when I interviewed Bob Precht, the producer of *The Ed Sullivan Show* from 1960 to the end of the series in 1971, he talked to me from his office at KECI-TV in Missoula, Montana, where he now resides. Precht, at that time, was president and owner of the station, an affiliate station of the NBC Television Network. The station also had two satellite TV stations, one in Kalispell and the other in Butte, Montana. The three stations reach a good part of the television public of western Montana.

Ed and I worked directly with Sol Hurok and the agents in his office. Hurok and the other managers were very anxious to place their performers or groups on the Sullivan show, especially if they were new American artists or European, Asian, or African artists who were new to the American audience. However, the agents and managers were not the only source for discovering great classical performers.

Ed Sullivan was constantly out on the town seeking material for his syndicated newspaper column, and he would be aware of what was happening in the entertainment world. For instance, if a sensational new opera star suddenly appeared on the scene, Ed would be there to catch the performance. Similarly, if a new Broadway show premiered, Ed would see it, because he was on the First Night press list. He was very aware of everything happening in the [show] busi-

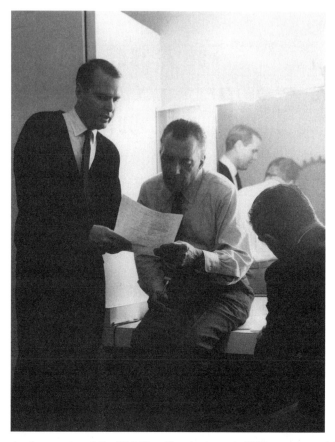

At a production meeting of *The Ed Sullivan Show* in the early 1960s are pictured (left to right) producer Bob Precht, Ed Sullivan, and stage manager Ken Campbell. (Sullivan Productions)

ness such as a new chanteuse at the Blue Angel or a break-through new comic at the Copacabana. A great part of Ed's success was that he had a "catholic" interest in the whole world of entertainment, which went from vaudeville to nightclubs to the classical concert stage. He covered them all.[1]

Precht then returned to his discussion of the agents and managers of the classical artists: "The artists' managers were constantly presenting their clients to us. They were good at marketing their clients, because the managers were aware that the Sullivan show was their only opportunity." By opportunity, Precht explained, it was their only chance to have their opera singers and classical musicians perform before an audience of millions of viewers of the Sullivan show.

The managers knew that if they had a performer who was unknown in this country, the best way of publicizing the performer was to have the artist appear on the show. Sol Hurok and the other manager would really campaign for their client's appearance. For instance, take the case of Sergio Franchi. Franchi was not a major opera star, but Hurok brought him to this country and arranged for Franchi to appear in concert at Carnegie Hall. Although his voice was not of the caliber of the Met [Metropolitan Opera] stars, he did sing well, especially the Neapolitan love songs and light classical works. He also was a charming man, and good-looking on stage. Hurok brought him to our attention, and we booked him on the show, and he did extremely well. For Hurok it was a major push. He was really keen on getting Franchi on the Sullivan show. As it turned out it was good for Hurok, and good for us. [Sergio Franchi became one of the Sullivan show's frequent guests and appeared on the show a total of twenty-four times.] So we had that relationship with Hurok, and less so with Columbia Artists, and some of the others. I know that the [William] Morris office, from time to time, also represented classical artists, and we had some of their clients on the show, but no matter who the agent was, Hurok, Columbia Artists, or the Morris office, they were aware that there was no other market for a classical performer. We were the major television platform for their talent. There was no other place you could go. Most of the Late [TV] shows would not book a classical performer, except perhaps *The Steve Allen Show*, and he wouldn't do that too often.

Ed Sullivan attended every opening of a Broadway show that he could fit into his busy schedule. It was a natural move to act as talent scout and present scenes from Broadway plays and musicals on his show. Pictured here are Elizabeth Allen and Sergio Franchi in a scene from their Broadway musical *Do I Hear a Waltz?* (Photofest)

Precht was aware that there were other shows that presented classical artists, such as *The Bell Telephone Hour* and *The Voice of Firestone*, but those shows were entirely devoted to classical music, and never achieved the mass audience that *The Ed Sullivan Show* attracted.

> Those shows appealed to a different audience. They were labeled, quote "classical" venue or show, and they had that PBS [which came much later] "feel." They were never on the level of share [of the television audience] that the Sullivan show was getting. And though many of the artists that played the Sullivan show appeared on the *Telephone Hour*, the show didn't have that popular appeal.

It drew mostly an upscale audience. But that was what the sponsor was going for, and they [the sponsor] were perfectly satisfied with. But the performers knew that *The Telephone Hour* and *The Voice of Firestone* did not have the popular appeal we had.

Another key to the success of our show, and why we attracted a large viewing audience was, of course, that the Sullivan show gave these artists only three or four minutes, or a ballet ensemble a few minutes more. It was important for us to keep the show [moving] at a fast pace. The classical attractions were sandwiched in among other performers of a popular nature and gave our show its interesting mix.

Another important point was that we never opened the show with a classical artist. Ed was very much aware that we had to open the show with an act that had strong popular appeal and grab the audience right from the start. Then, in the second half of the show, or even at the end of the show, we would present this wonderful piece of classical [artistry]. So the audience was there. They were with us. And also the audiences in those days were not as fickle with their remote controls. Once they were aboard the Sullivan show they'd stay to the end.

Precht continued comparing the programming of the Sullivan show to the lineup of acts on a vaudeville bill. "Ed understood that in vaudeville, you started slow and built to the big next-to-closing act. That went out the window with television, because Sullivan would open with the big act, and then bring back that big act later in the show for a second turn. Ed knew you had to grab the audience right at the top of the show."

When the Beatles first appeared on *The Ed Sullivan Show* on February 9, 1964, they opened the show, and later Ed brought them back in the second half for two more spots. In fact, every time the Beatles played the Sullivan show, and they made a total of ten appearances, they always opened the show.

For obvious reasons, Ed's busiest day of the week was Sundays, the day of the show. He often went from one production conference to another changing, adding, and cutting performers' offerings based on the reaction from the rehearsal audience. Ed is pictured here with the show's stage manager, Ken Campbell (left), and producer, Bob Precht (right). (Photofest)

If you go through some of the old show schedules, you will probably find that most of the classical or cultural attractions were in the second half of the show, but that didn't detract from the fact that they were there, and getting a good deal of time. Sometimes that was a problem, because some of these attractions—their pieces were often unusually . . . long—caused us to struggle to shorten them so that they could be worked into the timing of the show. Of course, there were exceptions as when we devoted the whole show to the Moiseyev [Dancers]. And even before my time [on the show], Ed committed to a series of programs with the Metropolitan Opera Company. And I think that was the only time that he, and the network, felt that he had kind of gone overboard, because apparently the ratings did drop. Although he announced that he would do a series of shows with the Met, there was some backpedaling on that, and the number of Met shows was cut back.

I think that Ed liked the classical arena, and he enjoyed the feedback. And I certainly did. It was great to be part of the culture. You felt somehow that you were doing something that had some importance to it. I am sure he liked that. From a social point of view, I think he enjoyed the cultural world—and the opera singers. It enabled him to have lunch with Sol Hurok, and that type of experience. I think he enjoyed that level of involvement.

I believe there is another person to take into consideration, and that is Sylvia [Mrs. Ed Sullivan]. Sylvia liked classical performers, and having been a woman brought up going to concerts, she, too, influenced Ed's thinking on this. I think the very fact that Sylvia loved to go to the opera and concerts, and would be enthusiastic about it, had to have some influence on Ed. Although I could never remember her urging Ed to book somebody. However, the very fact that she would go to see the Moiseyev, and get wildly enthusiastic and excited had to be an influence on Ed. Or that she was always willing or anxious to go to the Metropolitan Opera or a concert at Carnegie Hall must have impressed Ed.

It was common knowledge that Ed and Sylvia Sullivan were happily married and were seen everywhere together. She always accompanied Ed to the theater, a concert, or a nightclub, and it was not unusual for them to stay up until the wee hours of the morning listening to a nightclub singer. Sylvia was a very attractive, well-dressed, cultured woman. After each show, from backstage, Ed always called Sylvia (who watched the show on their television set at their apartment) to ask her how she liked it. He valued her opinions. They were a very close couple. When Sylvia died suddenly and unexpectedly of an aneurysm in 1973, Ed was devastated. Ed died of throat cancer just a year and a half later.

Precht mentioned that it would be hard to find a show in their regular series that had more than one classical act. "You could look back at the running schedules, and check it. It was the mix that was important. You must realize that opera was pretty special for the Sullivan audience, and although you could get away with it for three or four minutes, the audiences kind of accepted it, because coming up the next minute would be Topo Gigio. I think that Ed liked the cultural attractions, but felt uncomfortable if we leaned too heavily in that direction."

Turning to the supplier of cultural talent, Precht said,

Let's be candid about it. I think that Hurok looked at the Sullivan show as a powerful promotional device. I think he, and others, felt it was a good way of getting his artists national publicity. This attitude worked for Broadway shows as well. Merrick [David Merrick, the Broadway producer with the highest visibility of that era] used the Sullivan show as much as we enjoyed having the attractions. It worked both ways obviously, but they saw the value of the promotion. They got the national exposure, and we presented a wonderful scene from a Broadway show. But looking at it realistically, where else could a producer go with a Broadway show on television?

Precht also recalled an unusual cultural event on the show when he remembered artist Salvador Dali's appearance.

Ed booked Dali, and I shall never forget going to the St. Regis Hotel to meet Dali, and talking to him about what he was going to do on the show. He had come up with the idea of creating a painting by shooting at it with a pistol filled with paint capsules. He explained that he intended to express his art this way. It certainly was a different kind of cultural spot. He came on stage with the pistol filled with paint. Dali pointed it at the canvas, and shot at it several times. The colors exploded on the canvas. Dali had obviously created a painting in front of our audience. It was bizarre.

In conclusion, Precht said, "I am sure it's true that the Sullivan show influenced a lot of people out there who had never seen an opera singer or a ballet dancer or any of the cultural attractions. To have these attractions come into your living room with a guy you kind of trusted with your taste, like Ed, was important. On our show, you could see the latest act down at the Copacabana, but Ed also showed the audience what else was going on, opera, ballet, classical music, and Broadway plays. That had to strike some people, and even inspire some."

15

Sol Hurok, an Impresario's Impression of *The Ed Sullivan Show*

or the fifteenth anniversary of *The Ed Sullivan Show* in 1963, CBS asked classical music impresario Sol Hurok to write an appreciation of the show. Since the outset of the variety series, Hurok had been Sullivan's number one supplier of classical talent. During the 1940s, '50s, and '60s, he was the foremost producer of classical talent on a worldwide basis. His management office represented many of the foremost classical musicians, opera singers and ballet companies, and were especially adept at bringing foreign artists to tour America. The title "impresario" fits Sol Hurok in every way. The following essay is the one he wrote for the *CBS Press Book*.

It seems amazing to me that my good friend Ed Sullivan is celebrating his 15th anniversary.

How the years move on! But when one casts one's mind back over the incredible parade of performers who have appeared with him before his glittering curtain, this extraordinary number of Sunday evenings must indeed have come and gone.

There are many, many complimentary things I could say about Ed Sullivan. I've said a number of them to him personally. From my point of view, however, it is his contribution to the cultural life of our country that seems most important to mention at this time.

Maybe to the highbrow critic it would seem strange to cite the

Sullivan Show for Culture with a capital "C." But it isn't strange at all.

Planned by its producers to provide entertainment for the widest possible range in taste, for both adults and children, it has yet presented an astonishing range of major serious artists. Viewers amused by dog acts, acrobats, tunes from the Top Ten, popular movie stars, and athletic idols of the moment, suddenly find themselves confronted with Andrés Segovia, Maya Plisetskaya, Roberta Peters. It seems they keep on looking and, quite obviously, from reports to my offices in Kansas, Louisiana, Oregon, they often really listen. Of course, there are many thousands who have tuned in specially to see and hear these celebrated artists, but for millions more, I venture, this has been their baptism in the arts.

And for this daring venture, we can thank principally Ed himself. If it had been his alone to decide, I am positive that much more of the so-called long-hair music, dance and theater would have been worked in.

At any rate, through the Sullivan show America has seen such extraordinary events as the spectacular full-length Moiseyev broadcast, in which the whirling and leaping Russians captured the fancy of millions and brought a new surge of nationwide interest in dance. So impressive was this hour-long program that it was repeated in toto.

The seemingly airborne Margot Fonteyn danced a portion of the ballet created by the Royal Ballet for the Coronation of Elizabeth II. Maya Plisetskaya stepped from the Bolshoi company to ripple, quiver and die as "The Dying Swan." The great Segovia presided in the special silence he creates over his eloquent mastery of the Spanish guitar.

Time after time Roberta Peters cascaded her silvery scales and trills through operatic arias and songs. In fact, Miss Peters must have appeared on the Sullivan show as often as, if not more often than any other performer. The all-women Beryozka troupe from the Soviet Union glided through their patterns of its beautiful "Birch

Tree" number. Marian Anderson made a reverent occasion of one memorable Easter show.

These are only a few of my artists who have appeared with Ed. Many others equally impressive have struggled through the rounds of rehearsals and performed on one Sunday night or another.

And now on the occasion of this 15th anniversary I salute Ed Sullivan for all he has done and all he has tried to do. May he flourish on our Sunday night screens for decades to come.[1]

16

A CBS Executive Offers Some Insights into the Success of *The Ed Sullivan Show* and Why It Was Cancelled

In 1997, I interviewed Irwin Segelstein, one of the top CBS executives in the programming department at the time *The Ed Sullivan Show* was cancelled. He had an inside view of the mass cancellations of ten CBS series at the close of the 1971 season, among which was *The Ed Sullivan Show*.

Segelstein started the interview by talking about Ed Sullivan's appeal to his audience. He wondered what Ed Sullivan's "Q" score might have been. The Q score, developed in the early 1960s, rates the "likeability" quotient of a performer, and ultimately appeared to be very important to both the network and the sponsors.

Segelstein pondered,

We have to ask ourselves: What was the popularity of the show, what caused the popularity, and to what extent was that popularity due to Ed Sullivan himself? To answer this, we can look at the present day local news programs. Today, if you go to any local television station and ask them to analyze [the success] of their local news, very early on, they will give you the likeability scores, the Q scores, of their anchors, and their sports guy, and their weather man, and so forth. Because it is in vogue now to find out likeability. Apart from its content, what was the function of Sullivan's likeability? I now suspect that there was more likeability for Sullivan, the non-professional, and I mean nonprofessional not the unprofessional, by the people [the viewing audience].[1]

The executive continued,

Where the appeal came from, and what caused the likeability, I don't really know. And we don't have any research, but, I suspect that it was precisely because he was an "everyman" type of guy. Also, Sullivan, and a number of others [Broadway or Hollywood newspaper columnists] like Walter Winchell and Hedda Hopper and others, were accepted as "authorities" on entertainment. When Sullivan said this performer or act was "hot," they [the public] accepted it as a "given," whether they liked it or not. As long as he said it was "hot," they believed it. Probably, because he was also a syndicated columnist, he was accepted as an expert [in the world of entertainment]. So, I guess, in spite of the jokes made about him, his personal likeability made a difference.

Segelstein also recognized that Sullivan really had an instinct for what was hot in the world of entertainment, and pointed out that he booked Elvis Presley and the Beatles on the show just as they were beginning to be major entertainment attractions. He noted,

Ed had a "nose," an instinct for that "hot" celebrity. For that topicality, for that moment, Presley, the Beatles, at that instant Sullivan recognized they had the "heat."

As for the cultural aspect, I hardly thought about it during the seven or eight years I was exposed to the show. But looking at it psychologically, or perhaps it is more psycho-babble, I think that the three or four minutes of a high cultural performance gave the people some [personal] culture. I think it gave the audience the feeling that they were part of the culturally elite, just by seeing the performance. For instance, at Christmas, Sullivan probably put on a bit of *The Nutcracker* [he did several times]. The audience did not have to put in an investment of two hours to watch an opera or an Alvin Ailey or Martha Graham ballet, which might have meant boredom to them, but in three or four minutes [watching *The Nutcracker*], they felt like New Yorkers.

When the general audience appreciated a high cultural performance, they may have identified, on a subconscious level, with the New York cultural elite. Since the television audience was primarily rural, many may have wanted to identify with the cultural elite of the urban minority. *The Ed Sullivan Show* provided a possible entry point to this identification. To make this transition easier, cultural attractions such as opera singers performed popular arias from *Carmen* or *Pagliacci*, which are "tunes" the audience might have heard before.

The Ed Sullivan Show was cancelled by CBS in 1971, when Segelstein was an executive in programming for the network. He still believes that it was a mistake to cancel the show. The cancellation was based on the influence of demographics, which determine the qualitative aspects of the viewing audience, rather than considering the quantitative audience.

The Nielsen ratings have been the cornerstone of television ratings for more than fifty years and are based on the viewing patterns of a select number of Nielsen viewers from all over America. The television sets of the Nielsen viewers, whose identity must be kept secret, have been electronically linked to a central system, so that the Nielsen company knows exactly how many people are watching a particular television program, how long they stay tuned to the show, and what age group they fall into. Each Nielsen rating point is equal to approximately 1 million viewers. These Nielsen numbers are extremely important to the television networks and the advertis-

Ed Sullivan led the way in bringing country music stars to national television. One of his most popular guests from the Nashville country music scene was Roy Clark, the host of the popular *Hee Haw* television series. (Photofest)

ing agencies, because they determine the cost of a commercial minute on a particular television series. The size of the audience and makeup of the age group determine how much the network will charge sponsors, through their advertising agencies, to place their thirty- or fifteen-second commercial message on a particular show. Therefore, a television series with high Nielsen ratings will be much more expensive than one with lower Nielsen numbers.

> Why did CBS cancel the Sullivan series when it had a 36 share [of audience], is a question that still has not been answered. A 36 share was good in those days. Today it would be great. From a broadcasting view, it should have stayed on the air, but from a managerial and sales view, Skelton [*The Red Skelton Show*] and Gleason [*The Jackie Gleason Show*] all "skewed" to the older audience. The be-

ginning of the demographic "craziness" began to take shape. The sales department was saying to the management, "This [*The Ed Sullivan Show*] is not an easy show to sell." Bob Wood [the president of CBS at the time] came to us and said that the show [and seven other shows that had older audiences or rural-based audiences] had to be cancelled. My associates in the programming department echoed my concern when they said, "Where do you think we are going to find programs to replace these shows that can deliver the same high 'numbers'?" But management fought us on it, and the shows were all cancelled.

After *The Ed Sullivan Show*, *Green Acres*, and *Mayberry R.F.D.*, and other shows were cancelled, CBS took a nosedive in the overall ratings. For more than twenty years, the network had dominated the ratings for Sunday night. Throughout the 1970s and early 1980s, CBS lost that toehold on Sunday nights. It wasn't until CBS acquired *Murder, She Wrote* starring Angela Lansbury that the network regained its dominance of Sunday night ratings.

17

Larry Grossman, Former President of Public Broadcasting, Looks at the Cultural Impact of *The Ed Sullivan Show*

In November 1995 I interviewed Larry Grossman, who had been president of NBC News and the Public Broadcasting Service (PBS). I asked him about his contact, early in his career, with *The Ed Sullivan Show*. Grossman revealed that his first job in New York City during the 1950s had been at *Look* magazine where he was hired to do promotion for the magazine. Editors of the magazine believed that when the audience saw these celebrities on television, they would go out and buy the magazine. Grossman sought to place celebrities, who had been profiled in the magazine, on television to promote articles in *Look*. Since *The Ed Sullivan Show* was one of the most popular and highly rated programs on television, it was one of Grossman's chief targets.

According to Grossman, "*Look* magazine would not only do the 'pop stuff,' such as the *Look* All-American Football Team. If they had a 'highbrow' subject, such as a major opera star or famous Broadway theater actor or a concert star such as Isaac Stern, it would be important to place the personality on the Sullivan show, because it was the best showplace for promotion. In those days, there was much more of a combination of 'highbrow and lowbrow' on the show than we might dream of today."[1]

Grossman suggested that this combination of "highbrow and lowbrow" crossed over to other types of shows. For instance, the *$64,000 Question* television quiz show would seek to have a shoemaker who was an expert on grand opera. He notes, "There was a good deal of interplay between 'class' and 'mass.'"

As Grossman remarked, "At the outset, television was pretty much an upscale medium, probably because the wealthier people were the only ones who could afford to buy the television sets." He thought that as the price for TV sets became lower and available to all, the commercial networks began to cater to what they thought was the lowbrow tastes of the general public, the most effective way to attract advertisers.

> They began to go more and more down-market. So the networks gave up the "highbrow" shows, and there was nothing on the air comparable to the combination of the "highbrow and lowbrow" that the Sullivan show offered. For instance, there were other shows at the time. *Omnibus* was an ABC series. It was sort of a cultural magazine with Walter Kerr, the drama critic of the *New York Herald Tribune*, and Alistair Cooke as hosts. In those days, the medium was much more focused on "class stuff." But it was part of the genius and feel of the Sullivan show that you not only got the Beatles and the big movie stars like Martin and Lewis, but you also got the Itzhak Perlmans and the Isaac Sterns and the ballet dancers and the Metropolitan Opera stars as well.

When asked if PBS was affected by *The Ed Sullivan Show*, Grossman said he did not think so in terms of format. He added, "PBS felt that it was not in the entertainment business, which I think was a mistake. They would prefer to put on a whole opera instead of just a tenor singing an aria." Grossman felt that Public TV didn't learn from the Sullivan show to mix up the high and low culture. "There was some attempt by the late night shows, *The Jack*

Paar Show and *The Steve Allen Show*, to inject some high culture personalities such as Beverly Sills. But they often put them on because they were not only great singers, but good conversationalists and interesting people."

He said that even then, the networks did not want high cultural performers, because they felt that the growing audience was not interested in them. Variety television shows that followed Sullivan's show or were on during the run of the Sullivan show, such as *The Dean Martin Show*, *The Carol Burnett Show*, and *The Garry Moore Show*, did not attempt to mix high cultural personalities, on the whole, with the middlebrow and lowbrow acts.

It is quite evident that PBS has always strived to present high cultural artists and groups in their *American Masters* series and *Live from Lincoln Center* series, but there is seldom an attempt to mix high and low cultural acts in a variety format.

As Grossman said,

PBS's effort has been to present "culture as culture" such as the *Dance in America* series in which they present a whole ballet by the New York City Ballet Company or an entire opera by the Metropolitan Opera, not just highlights. The only time Public TV seems to move in that direction, toward a mass audience, is during fundraising weeks when they try to broaden their appeal and introduce popular events, such as national folk dance festivals, to attract people who will contribute money and support public television. When I was at PBS, we put on the Grand Ole Opry. It was the first time the Opry was on national television. It was so successful we had them on once a year after that. The audience seemed to love country music.

When asked if high culture and low culture might even be arbitrary terms, Grossman said,

It probably is. One generation's popular culture may end up being another's elite culture. Opera has always been for the masses in Europe. It still is today. Opera there is not only for the rich or well educated or for those people trying to show off their taste for culture. Here in America, there is a sort of snob appeal to say we are devotees of opera and ballet, but it is essentially not high class in Europe [or Russia], where it attracts a mass public. In our country, we never see a ballet on commercial television, while in Europe, ballet is carried on their commercial networks. It is surprising, in a sense, because dance is a very popular medium in this country. I think that the television viewing public in America uses television for relaxation and total escape, not so much for information and education and self-improvement. They get some of that, but the ratings tell us that they are watching the situation comedies, which are almost childish in their approach. Certainly the heavy television viewer seems to be on the low end of the scale. Paul Klein [former head of programming for NBC] said that viewers watch "the least objectionable program," and the ratings seem to bear him out. They watch because the programs don't raise questions or stimulate too long an engagement. It is almost wallpaper or tropical fish. It's something to watch and relax with.

Ed Sullivan, on the other hand, took chances. He put on the Moiseyev Dancers from Russia. But, in a sense, I don't believe it was a big gamble, because the Moiseyev could sell out Madison Square Garden. That's where I saw them. So Sullivan knew they could attract a large audience. One thing about Sullivan was that he was a newspaperman. He was always pursuing the news angle, as well as mere entertainment. It was because Moiseyev was such an oddity, as well as a great dance company, that it interested Sullivan. It was a curiosity, and he wanted to be the first to present them on television. When Sullivan first booked Itzhak Perlman on his show, he realized that here was a thirteen-year-old musical prodigy, who had polio, came from Israel, and was a master at playing the violin. He wasn't just looking for great talent, but someone who was unique and newsworthy.

Also at the time that Sullivan reigned, television was something new and wonderful. Just the mere opportunity to be on television was something new, exciting, and wonderful. And to bring these great names and artists to this new audience was an event. Today the audience is jaded.

Now with hundreds of channels to watch on cable, everyone can see cultural artists somewhere on television almost every day. The unique aspect of being on television has disappeared. And yet when the Sullivan show reappeared on television in the form of a series of specials called *The Best of Sullivan*, it did attract a large audience, and the reviewers embraced the show with plaudits they did not bestow on it during its original run.

Grossman said that during the early years of the Sullivan show, Sullivan "democratized" show business by bringing the stars of motion pictures into the homes. Before that time, the public, especially the rural public, did not have the opportunity to see the stars of the "big screen" up close. Sullivan brought Cary Grant, Fred Astaire, Bing Crosby, and dozens of other movie stars into the viewers' living rooms for the first time. "That's what Sullivan also capitalized on. He presented these legendary film names, and very shrewdly mixed them with the pop stars."

Grossman also pointed out that bringing opera into the mix of acts was not too great a leap in those days. He said that Rodgers and Hammerstein were on Broadway with their musical dramas, which, in some cases such as *Carousel*, was almost an operetta. Today, with rock 'n' roll, rap, and hip-hop, to put an opera on a commercial television network "would be a leap across great chasms, almost to another planet of a sort."

There's another thing that may be a factor . . . I'm sure it is a factor. In the days when Sullivan reigned supreme, the tone of society was set by the grown-ups. What was popular and important was determined by adults. It all changed in the sixties when the Beatles came over [to appear on the Sullivan show]. It was the turning point in many ways . . . the kids' culture took over. They bought all the records and tapes, and that's what we heard on the radio. It was the kids who became dominant. All the standards . . . and the basis for the standards were turned upside-down. It was the kids who determined the fashion and the music and the culture.

18

Paul Klein, Television Theorist, Discusses *The Ed Sullivan Show* and Television Viewing

Paul Klein, once the first head of research for NBC and later vice president in charge of programming at the network,[1] said that NBC was "amazed" by the success of *The Ed Sullivan Show*.

Here was a guy with a low "Q" score. Nobody liked him. They didn't dislike him, but they did not like him. The show had nothing that was attractive. Yet one act could do the trick. An act like the Beatles or Elvis Presley could do it. But you know, the only person at NBC who really understood it was [Robert] Kintner [president of NBC at that time]. He said it was the value of a "franchise." The audience, the people, are afraid of not going to the "franchise."

Let me explain it. Suppose you have a McDonald's on the corner, and you have a Smith's Fast Food on the other corner. Smith's may be far superior, but the people will go to the McDonald's because they are afraid to abandon the franchise. They feel that they are "supposed to go" to the McDonald's. That's a franchise. Now, little by little, the audience is being weaned away from the franchises, but they still go there. They still go to the "acceptable" show. The franchise is the show they are committed to. They spent so much time watching it that they feel they have an investment in it."[2]

Mr. Klein is known for developing a theory about television called LOP: Least Offensive Program. Klein believes that when people watch television, the program they turn to is the "Least Offensive Program" available. In other words, they put on the set to watch "television," and Mr. Klein believes that they select, what is to them, the show that is least objectionable. To Mr. Klein, *The Ed Sullivan Show* is a good example of a program that many people watched because it was much less objectionable than the other programs available from 8:00 to 9:00 p.m. every Sunday. He also pointed out that some of the competition achieved good ratings, for a while, but did not have the lasting power of the Sullivan show. It was the third network, the ABC Network, that suffered most. During the twenty-four-year run of *The Ed Sullivan Show*, NBC put many different programs in the same time slot—*The Steve Allen Show* and *The Colgate Comedy Hour* did best in the ratings—but ABC programs failed year after year in the 8:00-to-9:00 time slot on Sunday nights.

Klein doubts that *The Ed Sullivan Show* would be as successful if it came to television in the 1990s: "People accepted less in those days. I don't know if the audience would accept Señor Wences [a ventriloquist] or other acts of that type now."

Klein also said that Sullivan was watching the rating on a minute-to-minute basis.

> He could catch a "break" [a loss of viewers] when a novelty act made its appearance on the show. In those days it wasn't too important, because there was less switching of channels, since there were no remote controls. You had to get out of your chair, go over to the television set, and manually turn the channel. Even then, without having cable, when you turned to another channel, you might get a poor picture. Your reception might become "snowy." It was easier to sit and wait for another performer to appear than to switch away from the Sullivan show.

When asked about the high ratings that the Moiseyev and the Bolshoi achieved on the show, Paul Klein commented, "That's true.

But they got Sullivan's ratings. You could have put any show in that time slot, and it would have gotten the same rating that Sullivan got the week before. But you couldn't have done it two weeks in a row." He said that today you could put the Moiseyev in *Seinfeld*'s time slot for half an hour, and you would get *Seinfeld*'s ratings. "But you couldn't do for long, because the audience would ask, 'What happened to *Seinfeld*?' It works for one show. You can get away with anything if you have the 'franchise.' But not for long." Paul Klein explained that the franchise is like a habit. He added, "The franchise is like a road you take to work each day. You are 'comfortable' taking that road, so you don't look for any other road. But eventually you may have to look for a new road. Your road might become unpassable and you have to take a detour.

"A franchise exists because sometimes no one wants to throw any other programs against it. And maybe rightly so. There are fewer franchises now. *Seinfeld* is a franchise and *ER* even more so. But it's more difficult now to establish a franchise."

With cable, there are more choices. Therefore, it is harder to establish a franchise, and they are more fragile than the old franchises of *The Lucy Show* or *The Ed Sullivan Show*.

Klein added, "It's amazing how long the Sullivan show was on the air, and how short was the run of *The Dick Van Dyke Show*— five years." He thought it might be that *The Ed Sullivan Show* began in 1948 (as a local show in New York), and built its franchise early in the game.

"After the show became national," noted Klein, "and acquired more than two hundred stations, *The Ed Sullivan Show* began to really do well, because it reached a large audience that had never seen these types of performers [film stars, opera singers, ballet dancers, classical musicians]. It was the first time they saw these acts, and that was where his big audience was. Sullivan became big then, really big. The rural audience hadn't seen classical entertainment or anything like that. It was all new to them. Everyone watched Sullivan. What else was there to do? You watched television or did nothing at all."

Like Larry Grossman, Klein feels that the early television audience was upscale, and as television became more widespread, it began to reach a more downscale audience. However, this audience had never seen a ballet or opera of a classical pianist such as Eugene List. So Sullivan held the upscale audience, added the new downscale audience, and attracted an even larger total audience.

19

Alvin Cooperman, Television and Broadway Producer, Takes an In-Depth Look at *The Ed Sullivan Show*

Alvin Cooperman was a veteran producer, writer, and executive in the television and theatrical field. He won Emmy and Peabody awards for his television productions and was associated with some of the most acclaimed cultural television specials. Three NBC Television specials he produced, under the title *Live from Studio 8H*, won several Emmys in the 1980s. In the first, he presented *A Tribute to Toscanini* with violinist Itzhak Perlman, singer Leontyne Price, and Zubin Mehta and the New York Philharmonic. The second special was titled *An Evening with Jerome Robbins Ballet* featuring the famed choreographer Robbins and the New York City Ballet Company. The third and final special was *Caruso Remembered* starring Placido Domingo and Zubin Mehta and the New York Philharmonic. These television specials were presented in early 1982, 1983, and 1984. Cooperman was the president of Madison Square Garden and Madison Square Garden Productions, as well as the executive director of the Shubert Theater chain in New York.

I interviewed him in January 1997.

Cooperman's first job was with the Shubert Theaters and he

worked for them from 1939 (when he was sixteen years old) until 1952. The Shuberts—Lee, J.J., and John—treated him like a son, but he left because they stopped producing Broadway plays. Cooperman then joined the NBC Television Company and was assigned to the *Texaco Star Theater Show* starring Milton Berle (many referred to the program as "The Milton Berle Show," but it was not the official title).

Copperman recalled,

At NBC I was interviewed by Robert Sarnoff and assigned to the *Texaco Star Theater*. At that time, I didn't know a microphone from a camera. I did the Berle show for three years, which was an incredible experience, because Milton is one of the most knowledgeable theatrical men I have ever met.

I knew Ed Sullivan because he was a friend of Lee Shuberts's, and they used to dine together. I was not in their company, but I knew him. In fact, I think it was in 1956, when Sullivan brought together one hundred prominent television people, including me, and we established the Television Academy [the organization that selects the nominees and bestows the Emmy Awards], which is now called NATAS [National Academy of Television Arts and Sciences]. And, of course, I worked for "Pat" Weaver. [Sylvester "Pat" Weaver was president of NBC Television.]

Weaver believed that you have to, in the context of television programming, create "little drops of culture." And even though the ratings were not very good, if you continue those drops, ultimately, you will build an audience. That theory is a good one, and it worked for Ed Sullivan. Sullivan may not have expressed it as Pat [Weaver] did, but he used the "culture drops" formula on almost every show. He had an array of [cultural acts] opera stars and ballet dancers on his show, but it was all 'couched' in entertainment. For instance, some young person [viewing the show] would see Leontyne Price or Nureyev, and would be stunned by the talent, and by the visual beauty and sound of the music. But Sullivan did not give them a whole opera. Perhaps just an aria, or a piece of an aria, so that the young person could digest it and let it sit with them as they watched the popular acts, the comedians, the variety acts that filled out the rest of the program.

Pat Weaver believed that if a television network would take an hour—or in those years it was ninety minutes—for a television special, and maybe, twice a year, present classical programming, whether it be drama or music or dance, that that would somehow create a "blood flow" within the public that could be built up, and by continuing this type of programming for four or five years, the ratings would increase, because the viewing audience would increase [because of the blood flow] and they would like it. Unfortunately, there are no Pat Weavers around today. The networks don't give a damn about the public, and the public responds to whatever is put on. It's kind of a "Catch 22." You can't totally blame the networks. The public makes their demands by watching. On the other hand, Pat Weaver's theory and Ed Sullivan's, too, was that if you give them [the viewing public] a little bit, not a lot, a little bit [of cultural programming], and continue it over a period of time, you can build up an appetite for better quality shows.[1]

On occasion, Sullivan offered more than just a few minutes. In 1963, he gave the Obratsov Puppet Theater an entire show, all sixty minutes. When asked if the appearance of the Obratsov Puppets helped at the box office, Cooperman said quickly, "Obviously, it was very good for business. And don't forget," he added, "Sullivan had a newspaper column, as well, and that was important too."

Cooperman offered this personal observation:

Sullivan was unlike most columnists, such as [Walter] Winchell— and I worked with Winchell when he was the narrator for *The Untouchables* [Cooperman was the producer of this popular television series]. They [the columnists] were a bunch of hard-nosed guys. But Sullivan was not. Sullivan was a very compassionate man, and when it came to good things, whether pop or classical, he had a "good nose" for what was good, what was right.

I also had contact with Ed Sullivan when he hosted a television special I wrote called *Clownaround*. It was produced by Ed Sullivan's production company, Sullivan Productions, and staged by Gene Kelly. Moose Charlap wrote the music and I did the book and lyrics. Lucie Arnaz starred in it, with Ed Sullivan, who was in full clown makeup and costume.

The picture of Ed Sullivan in clown makeup, and dressed as a traditional clown, ran in hundreds of newspapers, and the show did well in the ratings.

"I had another contact with Sullivan in 1963. When John Shubert died," continued Cooperman.

I came back to run the Shubert Theaters. At that time, Vivien Leigh was starring in a play at our Majestic Theater called *Tovarich*. The play received modest reviews, but was not doing too well. To give the show more publicity, I suggested that Vivien do the little song and dance number that she did in the play on *The Ed Sullivan Show*. I called and spoke to Ed and Bob [Precht], and they said that they would love to have her on the show. But Vivien wouldn't do it. She was staying at the Sherry Netherland or the Plaza, I can't remember which, but I went over to the hotel and visited her. I told her how important an appearance on the Sullivan show could be for the show, and convinced her to do it. And the very next day after her appearance on the Sullivan show, you could see it at the box office. It gave the show a lift.[2]

Cooperman offered this insight about television and high cultural attractions: "There was a moment in time when people in the

The *Clownaround* special was broadcast on March 26, 1973. Sullivan appeared with Lucie Arnaz, Tiny Tim, and many of the best circus performers in the world. The drawing is by Rudy Cristiano. (Photofest)

industry thought that cable was the answer to putting the arts and culture on television. Bill Paley [the majority shareholder and CEO of CBS radio and television] started it with the Classical Channel, but that was short-lived—about thirty seconds. CBS had hoped the Classical Channel would be the PBS of cable, but it didn't work out. The advertisers wouldn't pay for it. It all boils down to the ratings."

Cooperman acknowledged his preference for producing culturally oriented programs. "Everything I've done has a cultural aspect. For instance, I produced Menotti's *Amahl and the Night Visitors*

[1978]. It starred Teresa Stratas and we did it at the Shepperton Studios in London. It was done on film. Arvin Brown directed, and we traveled to Israel's West Bank for the exteriors. We received glorious reviews. The NBC publicity director, Alan Baker, woke me up to read me John O'Connor's [television critic of the *New York Times*] review. It was a rave."

Cooperman lamented that there aren't more programs devoted to high culture on television today. "Take the Bolshoi," he said. "Where are you going to find a sponsor who would pay for two hours of wonderful music and dance today?"

Cooperman explained how difficult it is to even get cultural shows on PBS. "You have to have an underwriter before you even approach PBS. You also have to have a PBS station as your presenter. It seems to me that PBS looks more to BBC and other suppliers in Great Britain for their television series nowadays."

Cooperman had one last observation about *The Ed Sullivan Show* and other programs such as *The Voice of Firestone* and *The Bell Telephone Hour*: "I think that it was very important that they were done live. Not 'live on tape,' but really live. There was a certain excitement about live television that gets lost on tape. It was definitely more exciting."

20

Artistic Directors and Managers of Opera and Dance Companies Reflect upon the Influence of *The Ed Sullivan Show*

I n preparation for my doctoral thesis and this book, I prepared a survey to gather the opinions of how the cultural aspects of *The Ed Sullivan Show* affected the general managers and artistic directors of opera companies and dance companies in the United States. The survey also sought their input regarding the Sullivan show's effect on their venue, as well as the opera and dance audiences and performers they came in contact with.

The questionnaire package for the survey was sent to more than forty artistic directors and general managers of opera companies and to more than twenty artistic directors and general managers of dance companies. Enclosed were a cover letter explaining the reasons for the survey, the questionnaire, and a stamped-and-addressed return envelope.

Although the questionnaire (see appendix D) was sent out just prior to the Christmas season in 1996, I found that the response was immediate. Even more encouraging was the response rate (over 33 percent), much more than could be expected. The comments proved to be both informative and enlightening. Most of the directors answered the questions in great detail, though a few had been too young to have witnessed *The Ed Sullivan Show*.

One of the most revealing responses came from Janice Mancini Del Sesto, general director of the Boston Lyric Opera Company. To the question about the influence of the Sullivan show on her, she wrote, "It opened up the world of classical art and artists that were not available in live performances in my small hometown."

To the question about cultural artists who spoke to her about the Sullivan show, Ms. Del Sesto noted, "Yes [to the Sullivan show] and that of the *Firestone Hour*. Several (of the opera singers) have said it [was in] their interest and pursuit was initiated as a result." Ms. Del Sesto added, "Exposure to the 'high' arts through mass media is critical to the development of interest in new audiences. *The Ed Sullivan Show, Firestone Hour* and other programming of cultural attractions exposed and inspired potential audiences and talent."

In her answer to the questionnaire, Sue MacLennan, acting director of the Tri-Cities Opera Company based in Binghamton, New York, reinforced Ms. Del Sesto's remarks. She wrote that she watched *The Ed Sullivan Show* every week and "enjoyed them very much. It exposed me to an art form not available otherwise." And to the question about the Sullivan show influencing the audience to attend high cultural events, Ms. MacLennan wrote an emphatic "Yes!" adding that the Tri-Cities Opera "moved to a bigger theatre because they needed the space."

Ms. MacLennan concluded with this observation: "I was a very young person watching *The Ed Sullivan Show* with my family. I believe, because of the Sullivan show we were exposed to music that we would never had [sic] experienced. The arts are so available to us now; we wouldn't give a second thought. It made the way for many artists."

James Caraher, artistic director of the Indianapolis Opera Company, watched the Sullivan show "almost every week without fail." About the high cultural performers, Caraher remarked, "I looked forward to those performers weekly."

To the question about conversations with cultural artists and *The Ed Sullivan Show*'s effect on them, Mr. Caraher answered, "A few of my opera singer friends from my generation will occasionally ask: 'Do you remember so and so on the Ed Sullivan Show?' So it at least made an impression." To the question of whether the Sullivan show helped increase attendance at cultural events, Mr. Caraher wrote, "I am sure that the weekly exposure must have encouraged some interest where it may not have otherwise been. So I would expect attendance to increase somewhat." And in conclusion he stated, "I think it wonderful and probably very important for cultural 'acts' to be included with comedians, rock stars, jugglers, pop artists, etc., and went a long way in demystifying cultural performers and helped establish a foundation for the arts to grow and be appreciated in this country."

William Walker, general director of the Fort Worth Opera company, noted that the Sullivan show presented cultural artists that were the finest performers of the day. "Yes, the opera singers were always those at the very top." He also seconded the notion that the Sullivan show increased the interest in and attendance at high cultural events. The particular artists Walker recalled seeing included Robert Merrill, Cesare Siepi, Roberta Peters, Isaac Stern, and Van Cliburn.

David Bamberger, general director of the Cleveland Opera Company, acknowledged that the Sullivan show did have an influence on him and particularly remembered John Raitt in *Carousel*, Roberta Peters and Cesare Siepi as "Boris." Mr. Bamberger remarked that the show "was a good thing, before art got segregated to PBS." And added, "I also remember Señor Wences!" (a ventriloquist who appeared often on the Sullivan show).

Concerning the influence of the Sullivan show on increasing attendance, David Mallette, executive director of the Fort Worth-Dallas Ballet, answered, "No doubt the show had immense impact on the American cultural scene." He also mentioned that he had seen the show only rarely because "the show aired on Sunday evenings. My dad was a Baptist minister, we were in church!"

General managers and directors of opera and dance companies who replied to the survey worried that in recent years, audiences for the arts have been dwindling. Some of the directors and managers wondered, "Where will the new audiences come from?" The executive director of the Cincinnati Ballet, Kathleen Delaura, lamented, "I wish there was someone who could carry on his [Sullivan's] work into the next century. Larry Sterner, executive director of the Pennsylvania Ballet, based in Philadelphia, affirmed that the Sullivan show increased interest in and attendance at high cultural events and had an influence on directing some viewers toward a career in the performing arts. He commented that the show "was the first opportunity for a broad spectrum of American people to experience a sample of high culture through their television."

Martin Cohen, the general manager of the State Ballet of Missouri in Kansas City, wrote, "I have a memory of watching the show regularly, and remember the 'variety' aspect including the performing arts." As to its influence on the attendance of high cultural events, Mr. Cohen noted, "I believe it was a contributory factor as much as the overall changes in population and the search for community identity in the 50s and 60s." He added that he had several conversations with artists who have performed on the program (primarily New York City Ballet dancers) and "who speak fondly of those performances." In conclusion, Mr. Cohen noted that the show offered "a wonderful cultural balance, in the broadest sense of that phrase."

Dr. Karen Borchers, executive director of the Florida Ballet based in West Palm Beach, was more cautious in her answer, stating that the Sullivan show "possibly" had an effect in increasing attendance at cultural events. But she also added, "I think it was a positive thing to have done."

The executive director of the Pittsburgh Civic Light Opera, Charles Gray, indicated that *The Ed Sullivan Show*'s cultural presentations had a great influence on him. He wrote, "I, like many other young viewers, was led to accept and appreciate opera, ballet and classical musicians and performers as a natural part of the performing arts spectrum." Mr. Gray commented that a few artists had told him the show did influence their desire to pursue a career in opera and other high arts. According to Gray, *The Ed Sullivan Show* "did a good job in presenting the breadth of performing artists—from the highest, or most elite, to the most popular. How can you know what you like, or what is best, without being exposed to the whole gamut, from top to bottom?"

Phil Crosby, managing director of the Richmond (Virginia) Ballet, stated that when he watched *The Ed Sullivan Show* as a child, he was interested in the opera singers and ballet groups, though he "was always more interested in the comics, Broadway segments, and of course, Topo Gigio."

Writing about the show's effect on his career choice, Mr. Crosby acknowledged, "There must have been a large impact. My parents did not take me to opera or ballet as a child, but I have distinct memories of Joan Sutherland and Nureyev and Fonteyn directly from the Sullivan show."

To the question "Did the Sullivan show have an influence on you?" Peter Mark, general director of the Virginia Opera in Norfolk, Virginia, answered, "Absolutely!" and to the question "Did the Sullivan show have an influence in increasing the attendance of high cultural venues?" he responded, "Absolutely certain." Mr. Mark added that he misses the show "terribly." In a P.S. he added, "I was on the show in 1955 as a boys soprano live from the 70th Anniversary of the Metropolitan Opera."

The general director of the Chicago Opera Theater, Mark Tiarks, was very young when he "watched the show during the middle and early '60s when I was in grade school." He remarks, "I remember the high culture performers only vaguely although I'm

Sullivan presented the world-famous ballet team of Nureyev and Fonteyn on his show only one year after Rudolf Nureyev defected from Russia. (Photofest)

sure it had an effect (positive) on my later interest in music and opera. (Mostly I remember Señor Wences and Topo Gigio.)"

Mr. Tiarks remarked that "Chicago Opera Theater was founded in 1974, and so it would not be possible to see an increase in attendance." However, he also pointed out that "lots of organizations started in the late 60s and early 70s, though, and the exposure of the arts got on the Sullivan show may have been partially responsible." His comment affirms the notion that the Sullivan show may have had an influence in the cultural flowering of theater and opera and ballet companies in cities across America. In his personal comments about the Sullivan show, Mr. Tiarks stated, "It was a great thing and I wish more television shows today followed suit. I also remember very positively the number of performers from Broadway shows who appeared on it."

21
The Critics Weigh In

Ed Sullivan was careful to book each show so that there was always "something for everyone," he often said during interviews. He was interested in having an act with high cultural content in almost every show, but the key word in booking the performers was always "variety." Only in retrospect can you observe the obvious intent to present a "class" show. Sullivan himself always sought to be a "person of class." Even though his roots were strictly middle class, Sullivan strove for the better things in life.

His clothes were custom tailored by the Dunhill on 57th Street, a store for the elegant gentlemen of New York City. His apartment was on Park Avenue. He drove a top-of-the-line Lincoln automobile, and when traveling, Sullivan and his wife stayed at the finest hotels, such as the Carleton in Cannes, one of his favorite hotels to which he returned year after year.

Such tastes were distinctive in his program.

A look at programs from a representative year, 1966, demonstrates that the show always featured at least one act that could be regarded as "high culture." On November 13 of that year, Joan Sutherland, the Australian opera star, made one of her three appearances on the show. The same program also featured comedian Stu Gilliam, the McGuire Sisters (a popular singing act), and the Marquis Chimps (a troupe of performing chimpanzees). The following week, November 20, Franco Corelli, a leading tenor of the Metropolitan Opera, sang an aria. Also on the program with Mr.

One of Ed's favorite British singers, Petula Clark, appeared frequently on
The Ed Sullivan Show during the 1960s as part of music's "British invasion."
Petula, who had two number one hits in the United States, including "Downtown"
in 1964, made a total of eleven appearances on the show. (Photofest)

Corelli were comedians Alan King and Henny Youngman, British
rock 'n' rollers the Dave Clark Five, and Burger's Animals, a mixed
animal act. On the November 27 show, Sullivan presented Fiesta
Mexicana, a group of folk dancers from Mexico, singer Leslie Uggams, and the Muppets. On December 4, Metropolitan Opera singers, tenor Jan Peerce and baritone Robert Merrill, sang a duet. On
the same show were the Supremes, actor and comedian Red Buttons, Gary Lewis and the Playboys, and the Harlem Globetrotters,

the entertaining basketball players. The next week, December 11, Sullivan presented ballet dancers Edward Villella and Patricia Mc-Bride as well as the Obernkirchen Children's Choir, who were in New York to appear at Carnegie Hall. On the same Sunday evening show were comic Morey Amsterdam and comedienne Joan Rivers, as well as singer Diahann Carroll and trumpet virtuoso Harry James, a true mix of popular and classical artists.

In a month of shows, Ed Sullivan had presented five opera singers, a classical ballet duo, a folk dance group and a world-famous children's choir. All of these performers easily fit into the high culture category.

It is obvious, too, that Sullivan surrounded the high culture per-

Sullivan, who started his journalism career as a sportswriter, never lost his interest in sports, and he often booked sports figures and teams for his show. Here Ed is pictured with the Harlem Globetrotters, the talented and hugely entertaining basketball team that challenged professional basketball teams all over the world. (Photofest)

formers with vaudeville acts, comedians, popular singers, rock bands, and animal acts. As long as opera and ballet were featured, the show offered new cultural experiences to millions of viewers, many of whom had never attended an opera or a ballet. *The Ed Sullivan Show* opened a window to culture, and this practice continued throughout the variety program's duration.

For almost all of its twenty-three-year run, *The Ed Sullivan Show* was in the "top ten" of programs on television. Year in and year out, Sullivan—with his unique talent for booking both high and low culture acts and constantly seeking celebrities who were hot in the world of entertainment—maintained the show's great appeal to the television audience. The show had "grassroots appeal," and the ratings proved it a winner in the all-important Nielsen ratings.

In October 1980, when the Sullivan show returned to television in the form of repeat shows in the series titled *The Best of Sullivan*, John O'Connor of the *New York Times* took on the job of trying to assess the variety series once again. Although the *New York Times* had not been as kind to Sullivan in its reviews of the show in the 1950s and '60s, O'Connor, looking at *The Ed Sullivan Show* nine years after its demise, wrote more favorably of the show. O'Connor acknowledged Sullivan's deficiencies—his awkward posture and poor delivery—but he also praised Sullivan's ability to book superstars not only from television and film, but all of the performing arts, including theater, opera, and ballet. Writing in the June 24, 1967, issue of *Newsday*, Barbara Delatiner concurred, in particular admiring Sullivan's ability to balance low and high culture on a weekly basis. She predicted that his show could continue for another twenty years, varying little from its established format. A replacement for *The Ed Sullivan Show*, she conjectured, would not likely be an improvement.

Delatiner's estimation was certainly accurate, as far as ratings were concerned. When CBS cancelled the Sullivan show four years later, they made a terrible mistake. Looking at it as a business decision, it was very bad, because the shows that followed could not maintain the Sullivan ratings and, subsequently, the revenues for commercials, which are based on ratings. And as top entertainment and culture—yes, culture—the following dramas and comedies were failures. It took almost fifteen years and a program called *Murder, She Wrote*, starring Angela Lansbury, for CBS to regain the ratings for the Sunday hour, 8:00 to 9:00 p.m., a time slot Sullivan "owned" for twenty-three years.

There are many clues to why the Sullivan show was a success. I tend to believe that the key to the success of the series was in Ed Sullivan's basic approach to the programming of each show. Sullivan was a newspaperman all his working life. He thought like a newspaperman, and he viewed his television show with the eye of a newspaper editor. Sullivan enunciated it this way:

> My experience as a newspaperman is the reason we've lasted. I approach the show and put it together the way a reporter handles a story. Because of my background, I developed an instinct and a sensitivity to public trends. For the same reason that every newspaper in the country ran the firing of La Rosa on page one, I grabbed him for the show. [Singer Julius La Rosa had been fired by Arthur Godfrey from Godfrey's popular television show, and the firing made headlines for weeks.] I knew it was the hottest TV news in years.[1]

Sullivan liked to say that when Ed told Milton Berle that he was going to host a television variety show, Berle counseled him, "Ed you're a newspaperman. Leave show business to me."

Sullivan also believed that the fact that the show was a live television show, not filmed or taped, was, in part, an ingredient of the show's success. Sullivan felt the live aspect of the program helped it retain its spontaneity and punch, and he stated so in an interview: "A taped program retains a certain earthiness. . . . [In a live show] a light will go out. Something will be said wrong. That's okay. I'd rather have something go wrong and let people know that the show is live than correct and polish the tape."[2]

The Ed Sullivan Show was always a live show except for the programs that were done overseas or for sections of concerts or Broadway shows that couldn't be presented on the Sullivan stage on a Sunday night at 8:00 p.m.

Sullivan was a believer in the audience's ability to spot talent, probably more than any other host before or since his show ruled the airwaves.

The routine of testing the show in front of a theater audience was set during the very first year of the show. Sullivan insisted that on Sunday at 1:00 p.m., the show that was scheduled to be telecast live that night at 8:00 p.m. should have a full dress rehearsal in front of an audience in his studio-theater. So each Sunday, an audience of over seven hundred people filled the Ed Sullivan Theater and watched the show run a full hour, without stops, just as if it were being telecast to a national audience. Sullivan and his producer carefully noted the audience's reaction to each performer. Did the comic get his laughs? Did the singer's songs win applause? Was the excerpt from a Broadway show a success? Did the classical violinist hit the right note with the audience? Everything was taken into account. It was the consensus opinion of the audience that counted. Although there were only a little over seven hundred people in the audience, Sullivan felt they were a microcosm of the nation, and what the preview audience liked, so would 35 million viewers.

After the dress rehearsal, Sullivan met with his producer and they decided which numbers "worked" and which numbers should be eliminated. It was not unusual for producer Bob Precht to have to tell a singer that his or her second song had to be cut. Nor would a comedian be surprised when it was suggested that he take out a minute or two of a routine to "tighten it up." On rare occasions, if

Ed conferring with Mick Jagger and Keith Richards of the Rolling Stones. For one of their eight appearances, Sullivan asked the group to change the title lyrics of their number one hit, "Let's Spend the Night Together" to "Let's Spend Some Time Together." (Photofest)

an act really did badly with the audience, it was taken out of the show. The performers were always paid, but Sullivan would not allow an act that "flopped badly" at the rehearsal show go on that night.

There were also pleasant surprises at the rehearsal show. Directly after the one-hour dress rehearsal, Sullivan would invite one or two performers to try out their material in front of his audience. One Sunday, a new young comic named Flip Wilson was given the opportunity to perform in front of the afternoon audience. Wilson was such a hit with the rehearsal audience that Sullivan decided to put him into the show that night. A few cuts in the acts were made, so that Wilson could perform his three-minute comedy monologue. Flip Wilson made his television debut that night. He was, of course, an immediate hit, and his career, sparked by that initial appearance on the Sullivan show, soared. A few years later, Flip Wilson had his own comedy series, which was a very successful show on NBC for many years.

Although Ed Sullivan gave many performers their start in televi-

Ed Sullivan and Flip Wilson. (Photofest)

sion, neither he, nor his producer Bob Precht, tried to take advantage of giving performers a step up into the "big-time." Sullivan Productions, which produced *The Ed Sullivan Show*, made no attempt to sign up performers to management contracts as a result of offering them the opportunity to be on Ed's program. Sullivan was indeed a star-maker, but he never took advantage of this position to build a stable of his own stars, unlike other producers of successful television series. Sullivan was just interested in *The Ed Sullivan Show*. That was enough for him.

Even the journalists who covered television did not recognize Ed Sullivan's contribution to high culture. Les Brown, who was one of the *New York Times* reporters and a TV analyst for the newspaper, edited a comprehensive book on television titled *The New York Times Encyclopedia of Television* (1982).

In the book, Brown acknowledges that *The Ed Sullivan Show* "became a Sunday night habit of millions of households and demolished dozens of programs that attempted to compete with it." However, Brown demeans the program by calling it, "essentially a vaudeville hour, which used animal acts and circus acts, as well as popular singers and comedians."[3]

The book fails to credit the series for its high cultural content. To be fair, there were far less circus acts on the series than opera stars. Perhaps Brown is addressing the *perception* of the Sullivan show and not the reality of its programming. Nor does Sullivan, as host of the show, fare well, described by Brown as "a wooden and unprepossessing performer given to nervous mannerisms and slurred speech." On the other hand, the book does acknowledge Sullivan's "showmanship, the flair for presenting performing acts when they were most topical or when interest was high. Typically, Sullivan was first to present the Beatles in the U.S., and he gave Elvis Presley his first network exposure when he became a popular music sensation."[4] But the encyclopedia misses the opportunity to state that Sullivan also presented the television debut of many classical performers and singers, ballet dancers, and scores of other artists and groups. Nor is there mention of the dozens of scenes from Broadway shows.

When *The Ed Sullivan Show* debuted, Sullivan's fellow journalists were exceedingly harsh in their criticism of Sullivan as the host of the show. John Crosby, the television critic for the influential *New York Herald Tribune*, was particularly critical of Sullivan's talent as a television performer. He reviewed the premiere of the show in June 1948 and titled the column, "Why? Why? Why?" In the review he wrote, "One of the small but vexing questions confronting anyone in this area with a television set is Why is Ed Sullivan on every Sunday night? . . . Mr. Sullivan is a persuasive fellow (being able to get performers for so little money, but) . . . if he has any other qualifications for the job, they are not visible on the small screen."[5]

One wonders if Crosby, usually a fair and very erudite critic, was not a bit jealous that a fellow newsman had mounted a successful show. (When Crosby later appeared on television, he failed, because he was a very wooden figure himself.)

To any outside observer, it is probably clear that jealousy in the newspaper business was rampant, too. Jack O'Brian, who wrote a column and was the television and radio critic of the *New York Journal American* during the 1950s and '60s, constantly criticized the demeanor of Ed Sullivan as a television host and rarely gave the program a good review.

Sullivan published a retort to his critics in his own column in the *New York Daily News*: "Public opinion, I'm certain, would agree that I've contributed more to television in its embryonic state than you have contributed with your reckless and uninformed back-seat driving. You belt away at performers and producers as a means of earning a weekly salary. At least I give them a gracious introduction and a showmanly presentation that enhances their earning power."[6]

Jack Gould, television critic for the *New York Times*, wrote a review of *Toast of the Town* on July 4, 1948, and was very critical of Sullivan's ability to host a variety show. Crosby never abated in his criticism of Sullivan, insisting years later that "Mr. Sullivan is notoriously and admittedly without talent."⁷ On the other hand, Jack Gould changed his opinion of Sullivan and on the show's eighteenth anniversary, acknowledged Sullivan as one of television's great impresarios.

In his book *Smoke and Mirrors*, television critic John Leonard said this about Ed Sullivan:

> The public loved him, the stars showed up, and his critics couldn't really attribute the success of his show to his newspaper column. Maybe in the first few years, Sullivan could and did bully people into appearing on his show, as [Walter] Winchell, Louella Parsons and Elsa Maxwell had bullied people on to their radio programs with the promise or the threat of their syndicated clout. But it quickly became obvious that Ed's TV show instead of some sort of a tithe entertainers had to pay to get a favorable mention in the *Daily News*, was a career maker; that television was more important than newspapers; that ratings were bigger than readers.⁸

Leonard remarked upon another facet of Sullivan's success, his identification with his audience: "He was so pleased to be where he was, as we ourselves would have been. If he had to leave town, he brought home something he knew we would like because he liked it; a bicycle, a puppet, a Blarney stone. From Scandinavia, Sonja Henie. From Israel, Itzhak Perlman. From Mexico, Cantinflas. From France, Edith Piaf. From Italy, Gina Lollobrigida. From Russia, the Moiseyev Dance Troupe, and of course, Rudolf Nureyev, paired with Margo Fonteyn. Like Woody Allen's *Zelig*, he made every important scene, but didn't put on airs about it."⁹

Although the critics might have initially been skeptical of Sullivan's ability to host a variety program, Ed ultimately had the last laugh. Though he never polished his delivery or smoothed out his demeanor or delivery, he honed the one skill most important: presenting an array of acts that drew audiences week after week. For twenty-three years, that was all that mattered.

22
Conclusion

Ed Sullivan was, first and foremost, a newspaper columnist all of his working life. When he took on the task of hosting a variety television program at age forty-six, he continued to write his column for the *New York Daily News* and the *Daily News*'s newspaper syndicate. Sullivan's style for booking and programming the show reflected the eclectic approach of his newspaper column. It was not just a variety show or a vaudeville presentation, as some had dubbed it, but more of a "living newspaper" presenting what was "new" in the world of entertainment, sports, and culture. Although Sullivan's first producer, Marlo Lewis, claims to have had a hand in establishing the format, one has to merely observe the booking for the very first show to discover the obvious news-oriented direction of the program. In addition to Richard Rodgers and Oscar Hammerstein, the lyricist and composer of a dozen classic Broadway shows; Martin and Lewis, the top comedy team of that day; Kathryn Lee, a ballerina; and concert pianist Eugene List, Ed presented John Kokoman, a singing fireman whose story had been in the news; Ruby Goldstein, a boxing referee who discussed an upcoming championship boxing match; and singer Monica Lewis, Marlo's sister. There it is: theater, popular music, comedy, high culture, sports, and news.

In his interview for this book, Bob Precht, Ed Sullivan's second (and last) producer, mentioned the link between Sullivan's programming and his newspaperman's attitude. Others also pointed out Sullivan's newspaper background influencing the booking of acts for the show. However, most viewers then, and especially today, did not know that Sullivan was basically a newspaperman and that he only turned to television in his middle years.

The Ed Sullivan Show was referred to by many television critics as "television vaudeville," but the programming of each show was exactly the opposite of the running order of a vaudeville show. In vaudeville, the star was always placed in the next-to-closing spot. The vaudeville show built the excitement slowly, with novelty performers—such as acrobats, jugglers, magicians, and animal acts—in the first part of the program. Interspersed with these acts were singers, dance acts, and comedians who had not attained the status of top performers. Usually the big draw, either a famous singer or comedian, would be slotted just before the last act.

Ed Sullivan turned this running order upside down. He was aware that he had to hold the viewers' interest, and so the star performers and the spectacular acts always opened the show, and they often closed the show as well. If the Beatles were on the show, they opened the program, and then Sullivan would bring them back later in the show to perform additional numbers. When Elvis Presley was on the Sullivan show, he, too, was the opening act. Sullivan knew that he had to "grab" the audience and hold them "glued to the tube," so that they wouldn't be inclined to sample a show on another television station. And the acts were short—usually three minutes for each attraction, then on to another act. Pace was important, and so was variety. When many writers and critics (in the later years of the series) referred to Sullivan as a "great showman," they were complimenting him for his ability to book the most exciting and newsworthy performers and then set up the running order of the program so that the attention of the audience never ventured from the TV screen.

Ed Sullivan and his granddaughter Margo Precht, three, celebrated the beginning of his twenty-second season with a giant cake. The opening show on September 28, 1970, featured Barbra Streisand, Red Skelton, Tony Bennett, and the Temptations. The cake also celebrated Ed Sullivan's sixty-seventh birthday, which, by coincidence, was September 28. (Photofest)

In February 1997, I interviewed Irv Lichtman, the assistant managing editor of *Billboard* magazine, the recording industry's major trade journal. Lichtman watched *The Ed Sullivan Show* each week for entertainment as well as to keep up with the activities of the latest recording artists. In 1955, he started his career as a reporter for *Cash Box*, the other leading magazine covering the recording field. He remarked,

> The images of the era are inextricably tied to their appearances on *The Ed Sullivan Show*. I am speaking about pop singers and groups, but the same is true for the classical artists. I remember seeing Roberta Peters, that wonderful violinist [Itzhak Perlman] and the Metropolitan Opera stars. Or take the Beatles or Elvis: whenever you see a documentary about them, it will always contain tape from their appearances on *The Ed Sullivan Show*. It documented the music of the era [for example, the Jackson 5]. The appearances stimulated record sales and interest in seeing the performers. It seems natural that the Sullivan appearances would build up an audience [for concerts and recitals] for both the pop and classical artists. It certainly had a big impact on record sales.
>
> When I got into the [music] business, the Sullivan show was the one to watch. It was the most important music television show for all those years.[1]

One could expect that the impact of *The Ed Sullivan Show* would be evident in the programming of today's cultural programs, but unfortunately that has not happened. Today, with the exception of public television, there is not a weekly television series devoted to presenting high cultural performers. Nor is there a variety program on the networks or cable that features a mix of popular and high cultural artists.

One of the main reasons for this absence of cultural programming is that programs, especially on the national television networks, live or die by the Nielsen ratings. Television is, and has always been, a medium for advertising. Even public television is now loaded with advertisers who prefer to label themselves as "underwriters," but insist that their commercials—the same ones that

The Jackson 5, one of many up-and-coming musical acts that Sullivan promoted, appeared on the program twice, first in December 1969 and again in May 1970. (Photofest)

are viewed on the national networks and cable stations—run on PBS.

Sullivan was aware of the importance of ratings back in the 1950s and '60s and kept his eyes on the minute-to-minute changes in the ratings. His variety series maintained a 34 or 35 percent share of the audience for most of its twenty-three-year run. In addition to his own show's ratings, Sullivan followed the ratings of his competition—the programs on the other networks that competed for the audience on Sunday nights.

As Larry Grossman, former president of Public Broadcasting Service, noted in his interview with me, even today the PBS stations do not regularly present opera, dance, and classical musicians on their weekly programming schedules, but program these cultural attractions as monthly "specials" such as *Live from Lincoln Center* or the *Great Performances* series. He also pointed out that the management of PBS stations use these programs during their "pledge weeks" when they ask the viewers for contributions. These funds provide as much as half of the support needed to sustain the stations, since the government subsidies for public television have been drying up over the last few years.

In his article, "The Best Seat in the House?" Grossman noted, "Now we depend entirely on public broadcasting to fill the cultural void. In recent years, public radio and television have been the nation's only consistent reliable source for performing-arts programming. This is a far cry from the FCC's original (if unrealistic) goal of integrating art and commerce within mainstream commercial broadcasting. Ours is the only country, whose public broadcasting system arrived as an afterthought, years after commercial radio and television had gained the upper hand."[2]

In the 1950s and 1960s, William Paley, CEO of CBS, and Sylvester "Pat" Weaver of NBC believed that it was their responsibility (and good business) to present some programs featuring high cultural attractions, but today, with the exception of PBS and a few cable channels such as Bravo, Ovation, or Arts & Entertainment, there are few programs presenting high culture attractions. There is no one who follows Pat Weaver's philosophy of presenting the public with a series of "little drops of culture," cultural attractions in small doses on a regular basis to build an audience for this type of cultural presentation.

Even though PBS presents cultural programs on a semi-regular basis, the impact is not comparable to Sullivan's because the audience for PBS programs is relatively small. While Sullivan's weekly audience could reach as many as 35 million people, a large audience for a PBS show would be 2 million viewers, and the viewing audience for a cable television channel presentation is even smaller, seldom reaching more than 1 million viewers nationally.

Unfortunately, it appears that *The Ed Sullivan Show* did not have a strong influence on future television programming. It was a unique show, guided by a newspaperman with a flair for showmanship, and was, in a large part, his personal statement. It was indeed Ed Sullivan's show, and he put his personal stamp on it each week.

While one could concede that *The Ed Sullivan Show* did not influence television programming, it may have made a significant cultural impact otherwise. From many sources, experts in the field refer to a "cultural explosion" in the late 1960s and early 1970s. It is apparent that there was a groundswell during those years to establish high cultural institutions. It might be coincidental, but the fact remains that this hunger for culture, especially in the rural areas, where *The Ed Sullivan Show* was most popular, came at a time when the Sullivan show was hitting its peak, and was seen weekly by more than 35 million people.

The survey I conducted revealed that not only did *The Ed Sullivan Show* stimulate interest in the fields of opera, dance, and theater in the performing arts, but it had a marked influence in bringing directors and managers of artistic companies and venues into the field.

It appears that *The Ed Sullivan Show* influenced performers, artistic directors, and managers to enter the field of the "high" performing arts. The visual and audio diffusion of culture through the medium of television, especially the high cultural attractions on *The Ed Sullivan Show*, encouraged some members of his viewing audience to pursue a career in the performing arts high cultural arena.

I am certain that when Ed Sullivan and his producers planned each show, there was little or no thought given to the possibility that *The Ed Sullivan Show* might be a strong vehicle for opening up and educating the general public to the world of high cultural entertainment. The fact that, except for special programs such as the Bolshoi Ballet or the Spoleto Festival, which were slanted

Marquee on the Ed Sullivan Theater for the program
broadcast December 10, 1967. (Photofest)

toward this direction of high culture, Ed Sullivan rarely devoted
more than three or four minutes of the one-hour program to ballet,
opera, or performances of classical musical artists.

Nevertheless, these classical drops of culture appear to have had
a lasting effect on the entertainment values and interest of the audience of *The Ed Sullivan Show* that still resonates, to this day, in the
opera house, concert halls, auditoriums, and even stadiums where
classical artists and performers like the Three Tenors attract audiences in the thousands.

Appendix A: *The Ed Sullivan Show* Ratings and Audience Share

Nielsen Media Research began ranking television programs in the 1951 season, so no data exists for the first few years of *The Ed Sullivan Show* (*Toast of the Town* until the 1955 season). The rankings provided are for shows that appeared in the top thirty programs for that year.

Season	Rank	Audience Share
1948–1949	Unknown	Unknown
1949–1950	Unknown	Unknown
1950–1951	15	36.5
1951–1952	Unknown (outside top 30)	Unknown
1952–1953	Unknown (outside top 30)	Unknown
1953–1954	17	33.0
1954–1955	5	39.6
1955–1956	3	39.5
1956–1957	2	38.4
1957–1958	27	27.3
1958–1959	Unknown (outside top 30)	Unknown
1959–1960	12	28.0
1960–1961	15	25.0
1961–1962	19	23.5
1962–1963	14	24.9
1963–1964	8	27.5
1964–1965	15 (tie with *Petticoat Junction*)	25.2
1965–1966	17 (tie with *Walt Disney's Wonderful World of Color*)	23.2
1966–1967	10 (tie with three other shows)	22.8
1967–1968	13	23.2
1968–1969	23	21.2
1969–1970	27	20.3
1970–1971	Unknown (outside top 30)	Unknown

Appendix B: Awards

During its twenty-three-year run, *The Ed Sullivan Show* received several awards and nominations:

Emmys

1952 Nomination, Best Variety Show
1953 Nomination, Best Variety Program
1954 Nomination, Best Variety Program
1955 Nomination, Best Variety Series Program
1956 Winner, Best Variety Series Program
1957 Nomination, Best Series, One Hour or More
1958 Nomination, Best Musical, Variety, Audience Participation or Quiz Series

Golden Globes

1959 Winner, Best TV Show

Peabody Awards

1957 Winner
1960 Winner, for Contributions to International Understanding
1968 Winner

Appendix C: *The Ed Sullivan Show* on DVD and VHS

Many performances featured on *The Ed Sullivan Show* have been collected in anthologies on both video and DVD. However, many of these titles are out of print (particularly those on VHS), and those that *are* in print are subject to change. Titles produced on VHS, such as *Great Moments in Opera: Treasures from Ed Sullivan*, may eventually be released on DVD. Used copies of DVDs and VHS tapes may be purchased through such outlets as amazom.com or eBay.

Some of the Sullivan shows were packaged in multi-volume sets on disc and/or video, such as those produced by Rhino and Sofa Entertainment, and not intended for individual sale. Others, such as the Time Life series, could be purchased in separate volumes, but only through mail order or TV promotions. However, individual DVDs or tapes from these multi-volume sets may be available from vendors working through amazon.com or eBay.

This partial list contains titles that were produced at one point by legitimate vendors (as far as could be determined). The name of the manufacturer (when available) is listed in parentheses after each title. Beware of bootleg editions or those recorded overseas by unauthorized vendors.

DVD titles marked with an asterisk indicate that the title has also been available on VHS (though not always from the same company as the DVD manufacturer).

DVD Titles

The Best of Broadway Musicals: Original Cast Performances from *The Ed Sullivan Show** (Sofa)

The Best of *The Ed Sullivan Show*: Ed's Outrageous Moments* (Sofa)

Ed's Amazing Animal Acts (Sofa)

Ed Sullivan Presents Rock 'n' Roll Revolution (Sofa)

Ed Sullivan Presents Topo Gigio and Friends* (Sofa)

Ed Sullivan's Greatest Hits: Rock 'n' Roll Forever* (Sofa)

Ed Sullivan's Rock 'n' Roll Classics Volume 1 (Sofa)

Ed Sullivan's Rock 'n' Roll Classics* (Rhino):
- —Disc 1: Chart Toppers Volume 1 (Top Hits of 1965–1967)
- —Disc 2: Chart Toppers Volume 2 (Top Hits of 1968–1970)
- —Disc 3: The Soul of the Motor City
- —Disc 4: Elvis & Other Rock Greats
- —Disc 5: The Temptations and the Supremes
- —Disc 6: Love Songs
- —Disc 7: Rockin' the Sixties
- —Disc 8: Legends of Rock
- —Disc 9: The British Invasion

Ed Sullivan's Rock 'n' Roll Classics* (Time Life):
- —Classic Smash Hits of the 60s
- —Fabulous Females / Bad Boys of Rock 'n' Roll
- —Gone Too Soon / Groovy Sounds
- —Lennon and McCartney Songbook
- —Motor City Magic
- —Move to the Music
- —Rock Legends
- —Sweet Soul Music
- —Top Hits of '68 & '69
- —Top Pop Hits Time Life
- —West Coast Rock / Sounds of the City

The Ed Sullivan Show: A Classic Christmas (Sofa)

Elvis Presley: *The Ed Sullivan Show*s (Image Entertainment)

The Four Complete Historic Ed Sullivan Shows Featuring the Beatles (Sofa)

Holiday Greetings from *The Ed Sullivan Show** (Sofa)

Inspirational Treasures from *The Ed Sullivan Show** (Sofa)

Lucy Mania: Lucy and Desi Visit Ed Sullivan* (Good Times)

Muppets Magic from *The Ed Sullivan Show** (Sofa)

A Salute to the Red, White and Blue: Memorable Performances from *The Ed Sullivan Show** (Sofa)

The Very Best of *The Ed Sullivan Show*: Unforgettable Performances, Special Collector's Edition (Sofa)

The Very Best of *The Ed Sullivan Show*, Volume 1: Unforgettable Performances* (Sofa)

The Very Best of *The Ed Sullivan Show*, Volume 2: The Greatest Entertainers* (Sofa)

VHS Titles

A Classic Christmas from *The Ed Sullivan Show* (Walt Disney Video)

The Ed Sullivan Show: Rock 'n' Roll Forever (Good Times)

Great Moments in Opera from *The Ed Sullivan Show*: Volume 1 (Kultur)

Great Moments in Opera from *The Ed Sullivan Show*: Volume 2 (Kultur)

Great Moments in Opera: Treasures from Ed Sullivan (Sofa)

Motown Gold on *The Ed Sullivan Show* (Sofa)

Appendix D: Questionnaire and Cover Letter

In December 1996 I sent out a questionnaire to more than sixty artistic directors and general managers of opera companies and dance companies. This was accompanied by a cover letter explaining the purpose for the survey.

Dear Director:

I am in the process of writing a PhD dissertation in the discipline of Arts and the Humanities at New York University.

The subject of my dissertation is the High Cultural Aspects of *The Ed Sullivan Show* (1948–1971) and how it affected Cultural Diffusion in the United States.

As part of the research for the dissertation, I am conducting a survey to determine the possible influence of the high cultural performances on *The Ed Sullivan Show* on cultural organizations such as opera and ballet companies, and the attendance of performances at these venues in the United States.

I would appreciate it if you filled out the enclosed questionnaire and returned it to me with your thoughts. I have enclosed a stamped-addressed return envelope for your convenience, or you can fax your reply to me at 212-000-000.

If you have any personal feelings about *The Ed Sullivan Show*, I would welcome the opportunity to talk to you on the phone. Please call me Collect at 212-000-000.

I had a personal connection with *The Ed Sullivan Show*. My

P.R. agency represented *The Ed Sullivan Show* and Sullivan Productions from 1963 through the close of the series in 1971.

This dissertation is a serious work, and has the cooperation of Bob Precht, the producer of the Sullivan show.

I hope you can find a few minutes to help me with this dissertation. Your cooperation will be noted in the Dissertation's Acknowledgements.

Sincerely yours,

Bernard Ilson

Each letter was addressed personally to the directors of the ballet or opera company, as was the salutation. Enclosed with each letter was the following questionnaire.

Questionnaire

Did you ever watch *The Ed Sullivan Show*, which was telecast on the CBS-TV Network from 1958 to 1971?

If you watched the series, did you take note of the high cultural performers? There was usually at least one artist of this type on almost all of the programs. By high cultural performers, we refer to opera singers, classical musicians, ballet dancers, and folk dance groups. If so, has it had an influence on you?

Some surveys indicate that there was an "explosion of interest in the arts" during the 1950s and 1960s. Did your company or venue experience a great increase of attendance during this period?

If so, do you think that the Sullivan show, exposing millions of people to high cultural performers, might have had an influence in this increase in interest and attendance of high cultural venues?

Have you had conversations with cultural artists who mentioned the appearance of opera stars or other high cultural performers on the Sullivan show as having had an influence on their choice of an artistic career?

Do you have any thoughts at all about *The Ed Sullivan Show* and its presentation of high cultural artists?

Your age _____ (Optional)

Thank you. We have provided a stamped-addressed envelope for your convenience in returning this Questionnaire.

Notes

Chapter 1

1. Bob Precht, telephone interview with author, November 1996.
2. Precht, interview.
3. "Plenty of Nothing," *Time*, October 13, 1967, © Time Magazine.
4. "Plenty of Nothing."
5. "Plenty of Nothing."
6. "Plenty of Nothing."
7. "Plenty of Nothing."
8. "Ed Sullivan Goes On and On," *Life*, October 20, 1967. Copyright 1967 Life Inc. Reprinted with permission. All rights reserved.

Chapter 2

1. Critics were rated by *Variety*, a show business trade newspaper, as to their accuracy in predicting the success or failure of a Broadway production.
2. Ed Sullivan, *New York Graphic*, June 1, 1931.

Chapter 3

1. My first job in the publicity field was writing column items. I was still in Brooklyn College when I talked myself into a part-time job at the Spencer Hare Publicity Agency. I had a knack of writing topical gags, which Spencer would submit to Winchell or Sullivan or Earl Wilson and attribute the line to one of his clients.

I worked for several other press agents after leaving Spencer, including Sid Asher, Virginia Wicks, Stan Seiden, and Joe Richman. This route finally led to a job at NBC Television in their Comedy Development Writing Project. There was another young fellow on the staff who also got his sea legs in comedy by writing gags for press agents offered to gossip columnists. He was a seventeen-year-old kid named Woody Allen.

Chapter 5

1. Bert Bacharach is the father of composer Burt Bacharach.

Chapter 7

1. Bernie Ilson, *Total Magazine*, 1989.

Chapter 10

1. "Close-Up," *TV Guide*, November 30, 1963.

Chapter 11

1. John Leonard, *A Really Big Show: A Visual History of* The Ed Sullivan Show, ed. Claudia Falkenberg and Andrew Solt (New York: Viking Penguin, 1962), 142.

2. Leonard, *A Really Big Show*.

3. Bernard Gurtman, telephone interviews with author. All subsequent Gurtman quotes in this chapter are from these interviews.

4. Leonard, *A Really Big Show*.

5. Susan Elliot, *New York Post*, February 12, 1988.

6. Susan Elliot, *New York Post*, February 12, 1988.

7. Susan Elliot, *New York Post*, February 12, 1988.

8. Robert Merrill, telephone interview with author, May 1996. Unless noted otherwise, all Merrill quotes are taken from this interview.

9. During those years Martin Feinstein and Mike Sweeley were also directing aspects of Hurok's P.R. Martin Feinstein later became the General Director of the Washington Opera Company, whose current director is Placido Domingo.

Chapter 12

1. Ed Sullivan, "Where Do We Go from Here?" *CBS Press Book of the 15th Anniversary of* The Ed Sullivan Show, 1962.

Chapter 13

1. Marlo Lewis and Mina Bess Lewis, *Prime Time* (Los Angeles: J.P. Tarcher, 1979), 67.
2. Lewis & Lewis, *Prime Time*.
3. Lewis & Lewis, *Prime Time*.
4. Lewis & Lewis, *Prime Time*.

Chapter 14

1. Bob Precht, telephone interview with author, November 1996. All quotes by Precht are taken from this interview.

Chapter 15

1. Sol Hurok, *CBS Press Book of the 15th Anniversary of* The Ed Sullivan Show, 1962.

Chapter 16

1. Irwin Segelstein, interview with author, 1997. All quotes by Segelstein are taken from this interview.

Chapter 17

1. Larry Grossman, telephone interview with author, November 1995. All quotes by Grossman are taken from this interview.

Chapter 18

1. There is another aspect of Paul Klein's career that lives on in the area of television advertising. Klein inadvertently created a blueprint for television advertising that is an unshaken model to this day. It is the "Youth Market Myth of TV Advertising."

For almost thirty-five years, advertisers have zeroed in on the youth market and the young adults as the "prime target" of their television advertising. The advertising professionals insist that the eighteen- to forty-nine-year-olds are their most important audience, especially the segment from eighteen to twenty-nine. This rule, and it is a rule in today's television advertising, is based on the unsupported idea that if a young person buys a product, such as a Ford automobile, he will continue to buy Fords for the rest of his life. Sponsors are convinced that if a young person drinks Budweiser beer that he or she will forever be a Budweiser fan. Logical? Of course not. But it is so fixed in the minds of both the advertising community and their clients that it is unshakable.

It can be documented that more people over the age of fifty buy twice as many luxury cars—Cadillacs, Mercedes-Benzs, or Jaguars—as do young people, but these facts are ignored by both the advertising agencies and the clients. Just look at the television commercials for any make of automobile, and you will see only very attractive actors and actresses, all under the age of twenty-five, tooling along in fifty-thousand-dollar vehicles. Did you ever see a Lexus television commercial with a sixty-year-old behind the wheel? Of course not. But it is the fifty-plus population that buys the majority of these high-priced automobiles.

And where did this all start? We can trace this so-called importance of demographic misinformation to the late Paul Klein. In the 1970s, Paul Klein was the head of the research department at the NBC Television Network. During those years, NBC was having difficulty in achieving high Nielsen ratings for its television series. NBC was always second to CBS, and some weeks behind both CBS and ABC. Since advertising rates are based solely on the size of the audience a program attracts, it was vitally important for a television network to achieve top Nielsen numbers. Klein, who was a wizard with numbers, discovered that although NBC was lacking in total audience figures, it did very well in certain age categories, beating both CBS and ABC in catering to the eighteen- to forty-nine-year-old crowd. Armed with these figures, Klein met with Robert Kintner, the president of NBC Television, and suggested that NBC mount a campaign to convince the advertising professionals and their clients, the sponsors of the programs, that it was more important to "sell to the youngsters" rather than the older audience. Klein suggested a theory that fit to bolster the importance of catering to the youth market. He theorized that lifetime buying habits are set early in life, perhaps in the lower rungs of the eighteen- to forty-nine-year-old category. Since youth was on the march in the 1970s, and the Beatles and rock 'n' roll were at their height, it seemed to be a powerful plan. Kintner bought the idea and NBC started to promote the proposal that the NBC "young audience" (even if it were smaller than the total audiences of the other networks) was the "target audience." Klein was aware that the advertising executives would like the idea of selling to a young audience, because, in the main, the advertising profession is a young field. Advertising has always attracted the young, hip college graduates; at least it did in the '70s. Moreover the people who were the "time buyers," at the advertising agencies, the people who actually placed the television advertising "buys" with the television networks, were youngsters and gladly accepted this idea that they were the target audience. Kintner supported this trend by buying new series that were aimed at his now important young audience. Neither the NBC network nor the advertising agencies tested Klein's "new rule" with in-depth market research. They did not want to dispel Klein's theory. It all worked its magic like a charm. In later years, when Paul Klein went on to be head of programming at the NBC Television Network, and still later when he produced his own specials and programs for the network, he joked about his demographic invention, but few in the advertising business cared to listen. It is now written in stone across Madison Avenue, "The young audience is the target audience." The fact that it is the older audience, and to be exact, the older women's audience, that has the most buying power, is completely ignored by the youngsters who still believe Paul Klein's demographic sleight-of-hand charade.

2. Paul Klein, interview with author. All quotes by Klein are taken from this interview.

Chapter 19

1. Alvin Cooperman, interview with author, January 1997. All quotes by Cooperman are taken from this interview.

2. When asked what kind of a person Vivien Leigh was, Cooperman said, "Sweet, wonderful, and just a little fragile at that point in her life. Now, having read the Olivier biography, I understand even more. She had an enormously successful career and was a vibrant woman, but this was in 1963, and she was already seemingly fragile emotionally. She was, of course, a very beautiful woman."

Chapter 21

1. Michael Harris, *Always on Sunday: Ed Sullivan, an Inside View* (New York: Meredith Press, 1968), 90.

2. Harris, *Always on Sunday.*

3. Les Brown, *The New York Times Encyclopedia of Television* (New York: Times Books, 1985), 416.

4. Brown, *Encyclopedia of Television*, 416.

5. John Crosby, "Why? Why? Why?" *New York Herald Tribune*, June 22, 1948.

6. Ed Sullivan, "Toast of the Town," *New York Daily News*, June 24, 1948.

7. Jack Gould, *New York Times*, July 4, 1948.

8. John Leonard, *Smoke and Mirrors* (New York: The New Press, 1997).

9. Leonard, *Smoke and Mirrors*.

Chapter 22

1. Irv Lichtman, telephone interview with author, February 19, 1997.

2. Larry Grossman, "The Best Seat in the House?" *Gannett Center Journal*, Winter 1990.

Bibliography

Bantlinger, Patrick. *Bread and Circuses: Theories of Mass Culture and Social Decay*. Ithaca, NY: Cornell University Press, 1983.

Berger, John. "The Cultural Snob: There Is No 'Highbrow' Art." *Nation* (November 5, 1955): 380–82.

Bowles, Jerry. *A Thousand Sundays: The Story of* The Ed Sullivan Show. New York: G.P. Putnam's Sons, 1980.

Brown, Les. *The New York Times Encyclopedia of Television*. New York: Times Books, 1985.

Carey, James W. *Communication as Culture*. New York: Routledge, 1988.

CBS Press Information. *The Ed Sullivan Show: CBS 15th Anniversary Book*, 1962.

Curran, James, David Morley, and Valerie Walkerdine, eds. *Cultural Studies and Communication*. London: Edward Arnold, 1996.

Dixon, Roland Burrage. *The Building of Cultures*. New York: Charles Scribner's Sons, 1928.

The Ed Sullivan Clipping File at the Performing Arts Division of the New York Public Library.

Frow, John. *Cultural Studies and Cultural Value*. London: Oxford University Press, 1995.

Gans, Herbert. *Popular Culture and High Culture: An Analysis and Evaluation of Taste*. New York: Basic Books, 1975.

Gramsci, Antonio. *Selections from Cultural Writings*. Edited by David Forgacs and Geoffrey Nowell-Smith. Translated by William Boelhower. Cambridge, MA: Harvard University Press, 1985.

Grossman, Lawrence. *The Electronic Revolution*. New York: Viking, 1996.

Gruen, John. *The Private World of Ballet*. New York: Viking, 1970.

Harris, Michael David. *Always on Sunday: Ed Sullivan, an Inside View*. New York: Meredith Press, 1968.

Hurok, Sol. In collaboration with Ruth Goode. *Impresario: A Memoir*. New York: Random House, 1946.

———. *S. Hurok Presents: A Memoir of the Dance World*. New York: Hermitage House, 1953.

Johnson, Lesley. *The Culture Critics: From Matthew Arnold to Raymond Williams*. London: Routledge & Kegan Paul, 1979.

Leonard, John. *A Really Big Show: A Visual History of* The Ed Sullivan Show. Edited by Claudia Falkenberg and Andrew Solt. New York: Viking, 1962.

Leonard, John. *Smoke and Mirrors*. New York: The New Press, 1997.

Levine, Lawrence W. *Highbrow/Lowbrow: The Emergence of Cultural Hierarchy in America*. Cambridge, MA: Harvard University Press, 1988.

Lewis, Marlo, and Mina Bess Lewis. *Prime Time*. Los Angeles: J.P. Tarcher, 1979.

McGuigan, Jim. *Cultural Populism*. New York: Routledge, 1992.

Naylor, Larry L. *Culture and Change: An Introduction*. Westport, CT: Bergin & Garvey, 1996.

Robinson, Harlow. *The Last Impresario: The Life, Times and Legacy of Sol Hurok*. New York: Viking, 1994.

Sontag, Susan. *Against Interpretation and Other Essays*. New York: Farrar, Straus & Giroux, 1966.

Spindler, George, and Louise Spindler. *The American Cultural Dialogue and Its Transmission*. New York: Routledge, 1990.

Toffler, Alvin. *The Culture Consumers*. New York: St. Martin's Press, 1964.

Weaver, Pat. With Thomas M. Coffey. *The Best Seat in the House: The Golden Years of Radio and Television*. New York: Alfred A. Knopf, 1994.

Veblen, Thorstein. *The Theory of the Leisure Class*. New York: Penguin Books, 1994.

Index

$64,000 Question, 140

Aaron Slick from Punkin Crick, 99
ABC, 27, 90, 140, 146, 197
Access Hollywood, 50
Adams, Lee, 55
Agee, James, 19
Ailey, Alvin, 135
Allen, Elizabeth, 122
Allen, Fred, 19
Allen, Steve, 28, 53
Allen, Woody, 171, 194
All the Way Home, 19, 104
Amahl and the Night Visitors, 153
American Masters, 141
Amsterdam, Morey, 163
Anderson, Marian, 100, 130
Andrews, Julie, 3, 108, 110
The Animals, 65
Anka, Paul, 109
Anne of a Thousand Days, 105
Ann-Margret, 69, 109
Arcaro, 7
Armstrong, Louis, 7, 77, 93, 99, 108,
    113
Arnaz, Lucie, 152–153
Arnold, Eddy, 56
Arts and Entertainment Channel
    (A&E), 7, 178
Associated Booking Agency, 93
Associated Press (AP), 35
Astaire, Fred, 3, 29, 108, 110, 143

Avalon, Frankie, 109
"Ave Maria," 7

Babb, Jack, 26
Bacharach, Bert, 48, 194
Bacharach, Burt, 194
Bailey, Pearl, 77–78
Baker, Alan, 154
Ballet Españoles, 26
"Ballets: USA," 106
Ball, Lucille, 110
Bamberger, David, 157
Barber of Seville, 102
Barnum, P,.T., 110, 112
Basie, Count, 77, 93
Bates, Pegleg, 77
The Beatles, xi, 3, 11–12, 57–65, 67–
    68, 70, 101, 113, 123, 134, 140,
    144–45, 169, 174, 176, 187, 197
The Beatles at Shea Stadium, xiv
Beatty, Clyde, xii
Bel Geddes, Barbara, 104
Bell, Bobby, 80–81
The Bell Telephone Hour, 122–23,
    154
Bennett, Tony, 78, 86, 175
Benny, Jack, 19, 117
Bergen, Polly, 12
Bergman, Ingrid, 3
Berle, Milton, 117, 150, 165
Berlin Wall, 87
Bernhardt, Sarah, 111

Bernstein, Leonard, 58, 98
Beryozka troupe, 130
*The Best of Broadway Musicals:
Original Cast Performances from
The Ed Sullivan Show*, 186
The Best of Sullivan, 7, 143, 164
*The Best of The Ed Sullivan Show:
Ed's Outrageous Moments*, 186
"The Best Seat in the House?", 178
The Best Years of Our Lives, 104
The Bible, 108
The Bible (film), 39
Billboard magazine, 175
Bing, Rudolph, 89–90, 93, 95, 99,
106
"Birch Tree," 131
Blaine-Thompson Agency, 115
Block, Ray, 29
TheBlue Angel (nightclub), 10, 120
Blyth, Ann, 110
B'Nai Brith, 116
The Bolshoi Ballet, xii, 3, 38, 43, 86–
87, 100, 130, 146, 154, 179
Borchers, Karen, 158
Borge, Victor, 98, 116
Borscht Belt, 116
Boston Lyric Opera Company, 156
Boyer, Charles, 108
Boyle, Hal, 35–36
Bravo, 178
Brill and McCall, 65–70
Brill, Charley, 65–70
British invasion, 65, 162
Britton, Barbara, 12
Broadway, 22, 68, 87, 115, 143;
actors and actresses, xi, 139; ce-
lebrities, 20; columns, 25; colum-
nists, 18, 20, 134; composers, xii;
crowd, 49; press agents, 25; pro-
ducers, 25; segments on *The Ed
Sullivan Show*, 104, 122, 126–27,
159, 166, 170; shows, xii, 9–10,
18, 20, 22, 55, 104, 119, 122,
126–27, 150, 160, 173; street, 5,
9, 39, 62, 78; theater, 86–87, 116,
139

Brooklyn College, 193
Brown, Arvin, 154
Brown, James, 77
Brown, Les, 169, 198
Brynner, Yul, 104
Burger's Animals, 162
Burnett, Carol, 113
Burns and Allen, 19
Burton, Richard, 108
Butler, Robert, 106
Buttons, Red, 162
Bye Bye Birdie, 55
Byner, John, xiii, 4

Cagney, James, 105
Callas, Maria, xi, xiii, 3, 29, 90, 93,
96, 101–02, 106
Camelot, xii, 108
Campbell, Ken, 120, 124
Cantinflas, 171
Cantor, Arthur, 19
Cantor, Eddie, 19
Capitol Records, 59
Caraher, James, 156–57
Carleton hotel, 161
Carmen, 89, 135
Carnegie Hall, 121, 125, 163
"Carnival of Animals," 106
The Carol Burnett Show, 141
Caron, Leslie, 108
Carousel, 143, 157
Carroll, Diahann, 77, 163
Carter, Jack, 110
Caruso Remembered, 149
Cash Box magazine, 176
Catholic Charities, 116
Catskill Mountains, 93, 116
CBS, xi, xiv, 5, 8, 23, 55, 93, 117–18,
129, 133, 135–37, 153, 165, 178,
190, 197; Press Book, 129, 195;
Press Department, 27, 28, 103;
Television Studio (50), xi, 5, 67,
124
Charlap, Mark "Moose," 152
Charles, Ray, 77
Chevalier, Maurice, 110

Chicago Cubs, 50
Chicago Opera Theater, 159–60
Chicago Public radio, 65
Chicago Tribune, 8, 47, 49
Chicago Tribune syndicate, 8, 49;
    *Chicago Tribune/New York Daily
    News* Syndicate, 19, 22
Child's Restaurant, 37
Cincinnati Ballet, 158
Clark, Petula, 162
Clark, Roy, 136
Classical Channel, 153
A Classic Christmas from The Ed
    Sullivan Show, 187
Clayton, Jackson and Durante, 16
Cleveland Opera Company, 157
Cliburn, Van, 108, 157
Clownaround, xiv, 152–53
Cohan, George M. 111
Cohen, Martin, 158
Cohen, Myron, 95
Cole, Nat "King," 77
The Colgate Comedy Hour, 146
Collins, Jerry, 55–56
Columbia Arists, 121
Contino, Dick, 109
Cooke, Alistair, 140
Cooper, Gary, 3, 105
Cooperman, Alvin, 149–154, 198
Copacabana (nightclub), 10, 120,
    127
Coquette, 104
Corelli, Franco, 102, 161–62
Cosby, Bill, 77
The Court-Martial of Billy Mitchell,
    105
Coward, Noël, 105
Crabtree, Tom, 86, 107
Crosby, Bing, xi, 3–4, 29, 53, 110,
    143
Crosby, John, 170
Crosby, Norm, 4
Crosby, Phil, 159
Cuban missile crisis, 87
Cugat, Xavier, 22
Curtis, Tony, 110

Dali, Salvador, 126
Damone, Vic, 116
"Danny Boy," 36
The Danny Kaye Show, 100
Danny's Hideaway (restaurant),
    33–34
Danzig, Jerry, 117–18
The Dave Clark Five, 65, 162
Davis, Jr., Sammy, 77, 79
The Dean Martin Show, 141
Deauville Hotel, 62, 64
Delatiner, Barbara, 164–65
DeLaura, Kathleen, 158
De Lavallade, Carmen, 106
Delmonico Hotel, 22, 23, 29–30, 33,
    37
Dempsey, Jack, 9, 16, 29
de Wilde, Brandon, 104
The Dick Van Dyke Show, 147
Disney, Walt, 3, 84, 104
Do I Hear a Waltz?, 122
Domingo, Placido, 101, 149, 195
Don Giovanni, 90, 92
Don Juan in Hell, 108
Douglas, Scott, 106
"Downtown," 162
"drops of culture," xii, 150, 178,
    180
"Dueto final," 102
Dundee, Johnny, 9
Dunhill, 161
Durante, Jimmy, 16, 110

Ed's Amazing Animal Acts, 186
*Ed Sullivan Presents Rock 'n' Roll
    Revolution*, 186
*Ed Sullivan Presents Topo Gigio and
    Friends*, 186
Ed Sullivan's Favorite Irish Songs
    (LP), 71
*Ed Sullivan's Greatest Hits: Rock 'n'
    Roll Forever*, 186
Ed Sullivan's Rock 'n' Roll Classics,
    186
*Ed Sullivan's Rock 'n' Roll Classics
    Volume 1*, 186

The Ed Sullivan Show, xi–xiv, 1, 3–11, 13, 15–16, 19, 21, 25–30, 33, 35, 37–39, 41, 43–47, 50–51, 53–55, 57–58, 60–71, 77–81, 83–87, 89–113, 115–27, 129–31, 133–37, 139–48, 150–52, 154–81, 183, 185–87, 189–91; high cultural aspects of, 8, 87, 89, 134–35, 141, 152, 154, 156, 158–59, 161, 163–64, 169, 173, 176, 179–80, 189, 191

The Ed Sullivan Show: *A Classic Christmas*, 186

The Ed Sullivan Show: *Rock 'n' Roll Forever*, 187

Ed Sullivan Theater, 5, 34, 37, 39, 62, 67, 84, 166, 180

Ellen, 50

Ellington, Duke, 77–78

Elliott, Susan, 92

Elvis Presley: The Ed Sullivan Shows, 186

Emerson Radio, 78

Empire Theatre, xi

Emmy Awards, 149–50, 183

Entertainment Tonight, 50

Epstein, Brian, 12, 58–59, 61

ER, 5, 147

An Evening with Jerome Robbins Ballet, 149

Fabian, 109

Farrell, Eileen, 102, 106

FCC, 178

Fibber McGee and Molly, 19

Fidler, Jimmy, 8

Fiesta Mexicana, 162

The Firestone Hour. See *The Voice of Firestone*

Fisher, Eddie, 108–09

Fitzgerald, Ella, 93, 109

Florida Ballet, 158

The Flying Zacchinis, 106

Fonda, Henry, 105

Fonteyn, Margot, 106, 130, 159, 171

Fort Worth-Dallas Ballet, 157

Fort Worth Opera Company, 157

The Four Complete Historic Ed Sullivan Shows Featuring the Beatles, 187

The Four Tops, 77

Franchi, Sergio, 121–22

Francis, Connie, 109

Franklin, Joe, 7

Frey, David, xiii

Fry, Christopher, 104

Gale, Moe, 93

"Galway Bay," 72

Garfinckel's, 71–73

Garfunkel, Art, 113

Garland, Judy, 113

The Garry Moore Show, 141

Gary Lewis and the Playboys, 162

Gerry and the Pacemakers, 1

Giants Stadium, 98

Gillette, Bill, 117–118

Gilliam, Stu, 161

Gilpin, John, 106

Gino's (restaurant), 22, 33, 37

Gioli, Anabella, 84

Gioli, Federico, 84

Gleason, Jackie, 136

Godfrey, Arthur, 165

Golden Globes, 183

Goldstein, Ruby, 21, 173

Goodman, Lee, 21

Good Morning, America, 50

Good News, 104

Gorshin, Frank, 67, 69

Gould, Jack, 171

Goulet, Robert, 108

Graham, Martha, 135

Grand Ole Opry, 141

Grant, Cary, 143

Graphic, 17–19, 50, 193

Gray, Charles, 158–159

Great Moments in Opera from The Ed Sullivan Show: *Volume 1*, 187

Great Moments in Opera from The Ed Sullivan Show: *Volume 2*, 187

Great Moments in Opera: Treasures from Ed Sullivan, 102, 185, 187

Great Performances, 92, 178
Green Acres, 137
Gregory, Paul, 108
Grossinger, Jennie, 116
Grossinger's, 93
Grossman, Larry, 139–44, 148,
    177–78
Gurtman, Bernard, 91, 95–102,
    194n

Halloran Hospital, 116
Hammerstein II, Oscar, xii, 21, 104,
    108, 143, 173
Harlem Globetrotters, 162–63
Harris, Julie, 104
Harrison, George, 58–60, 66, 113.
    See also The Beatles
Harrison, Rex, 104–105
Hart, Moss, 108
Harvest Moon Ball, 20, 116, 118
Hayes, Helen, xi, 19, 104, 108
Hearst newspapers, 8, 48–49
Heathrow Airport, 58, 62
Hee Haw, 136
Henie, Sonja, 171
Henson, Jim, 87
Hepburn, Audrey, xi, 104–105
Herman's Hermits, 65
Hill, Arthur, 104
Hines, Jerome, 106
Holiday Greetings from The Ed Sulli-
    van Show, 187
Holloway, Stanley, 108
Hollywood, xi, 9, 25, 55; actors and
    actresses, xi; columnists, 134; pro-
    ducers, 25; stars; xi, 3, 20.
Hollywood Reporter, 49
Hope, Bob, xi, 3, 108
Hopper, Hedda, 8, 49, 134
Horne, Lena, 77, 108
Hunt, Jr. George, 61
Hurok, Sol, 86, 95, 100, 101, 111,
    119, 121, 125–26, 129–31, 195
Huston, John, 39
"A Hymn to Ed Sullivan," 55

"I'd Do Anything," 68
Il Pagliacci, 102, 135
Ilson, Bernie, xiii, 3, 25–31, 34–43,
    49, 55–66, 71–76, 91–92, 95,
    119, 133, 139, 149, 155, 175,
    179, 189–90, 193–94
Indianapolis Opera Company, 156
Inspirational Treasures from The Ed
    Sullivan Show, 187
"I Remember It Well," 110
"I Want to Hold Your Hand," 58
"I Whistle a Happy Tune," 104

The Jack Paar Show, 140–41
The Jackie Gleason Show, 136
Jackson, Eddie, 110
Jackson 5, 176–77
Jagger, Mick, 113, 167
James, Harry, 163
Jet magazine, 81
Johanssen, Grant, 108
John Brown's Body, 1008
Johnson, Lady Bird, 71–72, 76
Johnson, Lyndon, 71–76
Jones, Brian, 113
Jones, Davey, 68–69
Jordan, Will, xiii, 4–5
Journey's End, 104

Kael, Pauline, 92
Kalcheim, Harry, 55–56
Kaye, Danny, 78
Kaye, Nora, 106
KECI-TV, 119
Kelly, Gene, 108, 152
Kelly, Grace, 104
Kentucky Derby, 7
Kerr, Walter, 140
Kilgallen, Dorothy, 8, 25, 48
Kim Sisters, 110
King, Alan, 13, 96, 162
The King and I, 104
King, Coretta Scott, 80
King, Martin Luther, 80
King, Michael, 108
King, Sonny, 110

Kingman, Don, 22
Kintner, Robert, 145, 197
Kirkwood and Goodman, 21
Kirkwood, Jimmy, 21
The Kirov Ballet (Dance Company), xii
Kirsten, Dorothy, 90, 102
Kitt, Eartha, 77–78
Klein, Paul, 142, 145–148, 196–198n
Knights of Malta, 33
Kokoman, John, xii, 21, 173
Kostelanetz, Andre, 105
Kutscher's, 93

La Bohème, 90
La Forza Del Destino, 102
La Gallienne, Eva, 111
La Guardia Airport, 62
Lahr, Bert, 105
Lancaster, Burt, 110
Lane, Ricky, 83
Lansbury, Angela, 137, 165
La Rosa, Julius, 165
The Larry King Show, 50
La Scala, 91
The Late Show with David Letterman, 7, 50, 66
Laughton, Charles, 54–55, 108
Lawrence, Gertrude, 104, 110
Leader, 17
Leddy, Mark, 26, 29
Lee, Brenda, 109
Lee, Kathryn, xii, 21, 173
Lee, Peggy, 109
Leigh, Vivien, 152, 198n
Lemmon, Jack, 105
Lennon, John, 58–59, 68–70, 113. See also The Beatles
Leonard, John, 89, 91–92, 171, 194, 199
Lerner, Alan Jay, 108
"Let's Spend the Night Together," 167
Lewis, Jerry, xii, 21, 104, 108, 140, 173

Lewis, Marlo, 6, 115–18, 173, 195
Lewis, Monica, 116, 173
Libidins, David, 26
Lichtman, Irv, 175
Life magazine, 11, 13, 28, 59, 61, 62, 64, 193
Lincoln Center, 91, 141, 177
Lincoln Mercury, 78
List, Eugene, xii, 21, 108, 148, 173
Little, Rich, xiii, 5
Live from Lincoln Center, 141, 177
Live from Studio 8H, 149
Live with Regis and Kelly, 50
Loew's State Theater, 20, 116
Logan, Joshua, 107–08
Lollobrigida, Gina, 171
London, George, 106
Look magazine, 59, 139
Loewe, Frederick, 108
Louis, Joe, 16
Lucy Mania: Lucy and Desi Visit Ed Sullivan, 187
The Lucy Show, 147
Lunt, Alfred, 104
Lynde, Paul, 55
Lyons, Leonard, 8, 25, 48–49

Mabley, Moms, 77
MacFadden, Bernarr, 17
MacLennan, Susan, 156
Macy's, 97
Madame Butterfly, 90
Madison Square Garden, 20, 116, 118, 142, 149
Madison Sqaure Garden Productions, 149
Madonna, 49
Majestic Theater, 152
Mallette, David, 157
Mancini Del Sesto, Janice, 156
March, Fredric, xi, 104
Marciano, Rocky, 10
Maris nuns, 116
Mark, Peter, 159
Markham, Dewey "Pigmeat," 77
Marquis Chimps, 161

Marsden, Gerry, 1
Martin and Lewis, 21, 104, 140, 173
Martin, Dean, xii, 21, 104, 108, 140, 173
Mason, Jackie, 28–30, 35
Mason, James, 104
Mason, Pamela, 104
The Masters (golf tournament), 16
Mathis, Johnny, 77, 109
Maxine Elliott Theater, 5, 108
Mayberry, R.F.D., 137
McBride, Patricia, 163
McCall, Mitzi, 65–70
McCartney, Paul, 58–60, 113. See also The Beatles
McGuire Sisters, 110, 161
McLennon, Rodney, 108
Meeker, Ralph, 104
Mehta, Zubin, 149
Member of the Wedding, 104
Menotti, Gian Carlo, 7, 153
Merrick, David, 126
Merrill, Robert, xi, 29, 91–96, 99–102, 106, 157, 162, 194
Metropolitan Opera, xii, 8, 89–90, 92–96, 99, 106, 121, 124–25, 140–41, 159, 161–62, 176
MGM, 116
Miami Beach, 62, 64
Miami International Airport, 62–64
Mickey Mouse, 84
Miles, Jackie, 116
The Milton Berle Show, 100, 150. See also Texaco Star Theater Show
Miner, Worthington, 23, 117–18
Mister Roberts, 105
Mitchum, Robert, 105
Mitropolous, Dimitri, 106
Moffo, Anna, 96, 102
Moiseyev Ballet, 38, 43, 86, 95, 99–100, 106, 124–25, 130, 142, 146–47, 171
Monet, 22
The Monkees, 68
Montealegre, Felicia, 58

Montreal Expo, 38–40
Morning Telegraph, 17
Moscow Circus, 38–39, 44
Motown Gold on The Ed Sullivan Show, 187
Mozart, Wolfgang Amadeus, 92
MTV, 7
Mulhare, Edward, 108
Muppets Magic from The Ed Sullivan Show, 187
The Muppets, 87, 162, 187
Murder, She Wrote, 137, 165
Murtha, Jim, 95, 101
"My Big Break," 65
My Fair Lady, 108

Nash, Ogden, 106
Nashville Network, 7
National Academy of Television Arts and Sciences (NATAS), 150
National Enquirer, 49
NBC, 5, 26, 53, 90, 110, 117, 119, 139, 142, 145–46, 149–50, 154, 168, 178, 194, 196, 197, 203
Nelson, Barry, 104
Nero, Peter, 96
Nevele, 93
Newfeld, Mace, 65
Newsday, 164
Newsweek, 60
New York Bulletin, 17
New York City Ballet Company, xii, 141, 149, 158
New York Daily News, xi, 8, 18–20, 22, 25, 47–48, 116–17, 120, 173
New York Daily News-Chicago Tribune, 22, 25, 47
New York Evening Mail, 15–17
New York Herald Tribune, 140, 170, 198
New York Heart Fund, 115
New York Journal American, 170
New York Mets, 7
New York Mirror, 17
New York Philharmonic, 105, 149
New York Post, 48, 49, 92, 194

New York Sun, 16–17
New York Times, 28, 49, 154, 164, 169, 171, 198
The New York Times Encyclopedia of Television, 169
New York Times magazine, 59
New York Yankees, 50, 91, 96
Nielsen ratings, 53, 135–36, 164, 176, 181, 197
Night of the Hunter, 105
Nilsson, Birgit, 94, 102
Nine Days a Queen, 104
Niven, David, 104
Nureyev, Rudolf, 150, 159–60, 171
The Nutcracker, 135

Obernkirchen Children's Choir, 163
Obratsov Puppets, 86–87, 151
Obratsov Russian Puppet Theater, 86–87, 151
Obratsov, Sergei, 87
O'Brian, Jack, 170
O'Connor, John, 154, 164
O'Keefe Center Theatre, 110
Oliver!, 68
Olympia Theater, 61
Omnibus, 140
Oprah, 49
O'Shea, Tessie, 67
Ovation, 178

Paar, Jack, 28, 60
Page, Patti, 109, 116
Paley, William, 118, 153, 178
Palmer, Lilli, 104
Parker, Colonel Tom, 53, 56
Parsons, Louella, 8, 49, 171
Patterson, Joseph, 19
Pavarotti, Luciano, 98
PBS, 98, 122, 139–41, 153–54, 157, 177–78
Peabody Awards, 149, 183
Peerce, Jan, 93, 95, 101–02, 106, 162
Pennsylvania Ballet, 158
Perego, Maria, 84

Perlman, Itzhak, 95, 100, 140, 142, 149, 171, 176
Peters, Roberta, xii, 8, 90–93, 95–96, 102, 106, 130, 157, 176
Petticoat Junction, 181
The Philadelphia Ledger, 17
Piaf, Edith, 171
Piccoli Theatre, 112
Pitt, Brad, 49
Pittsburgh Civic Light Opera, 158
Plaza Hotel, 61–62, 152
Plisetskaya, Maya, 106, 130
Poor Richard Society, 116
Port Chester Item, 15, 77
Porter, Cole, 107–08
Powell, Jane, 108, 110
Power, Tyrone, 108
Precht, Betty Sullivan, 29–30, 33
Precht, Bob, 6, 9–13, 26–27, 29, 33, 38, 39, 40, 45, 62, 65, 68, 97, 119–27, 152, 166, 169, 173, 190, 193, 195
Precht, Margo, 175
Presley, Elvis, xi, 3, 53–57, 59, 94, 101, 108, 113, 134, 145, 169, 174, 176, 186
Price, Leontyne, 102, 106, 149–50
Prime Time, 116
Public television, 7
Pultizer Prize, 19
"A Puzzlement," 104

"Q" score, 133, 145
Queen Elizabeth II, 59, 130
Quinn, Anthony, 108
Quirk, Tom, 28

Radio City Music Hall, 95
Raitt, John, 157
Ramey, Samuel, 92
A Really Big Show, 89, 194
The Red Skelton Show, 136
Rhino, 185–86
Richards, Keith, 113, 167
Richmond Ballet, 159
Ringling Brothers, 106, 111

Rivers, Joan, 163
The Road to Rome, 104
Robbins, Jerome, 106, 149
Robinson, Bill "Bojangles," 77–78
Rockefeller Center, 35
Rodgers, Richard, xii, 21, 104, 108, 143, 173
Rogers and Cowan, 26–27
Rogers, Henry, 27
Rolling Stones, 65, 101, 113, 167
Rose, Billy, 111
Rowan and Martin, 110
Roxy Theater, 95, 118
Royal Ballet, 130
Ruth, Babe, 15, 50–51
Ryan, John, 44

Saint-Saëns, Camille, 106
Sales, Soupy, 44, 83
A Salute to the Red, White and Blue: Memorable Performances from The Ed Sullivan Show, 187
Sandburg, Carl, 108
Santullo, Carmine, 22, 25, 29, 47
Sarazen, Gene, 9, 16
Sardi's Restaurant, 69, 117
Sarnoff, Robert, 150
Saturday Night Live, 5
Scott, Martha, 104
Secret Service, 73
Segelstein, Irwin, 133–137, 195
Segovia, Andrés, 95, 100, 130
Seinfeld, 147
"Sempre libre," 102
Señor Wences, 116, 146, 157, 160
Shearer, Moira, 106
Shepperton Studios, 154
Sherry Netherland, 152
Sherwood, Robert E., 104, 108
Shore, Dinah, 108, 110
Shubert, J.J., 110, 150
Shubert, John, 110, 150, 152
Shubert, Lee, 110, 150
Shuert Theater chain, 139, 149, 152
Shubert Theater Productions, 25
Siepi, Cesare, 106, 157

Sills, Beverly, 91, 102, 141
Silvers, Phil, 110
The Silver Slipper (nightclub), 16
Simon, Paul, 113
Sinatra, Frank, 53, 86
singing fireman. *See* Kokoman, John
Skelton, Red, 113, 136, 175
Skolsky, Sidney, 8, 48
Sleeping Beauty, 106
Smith, Kate, 109
Smith, Liz, 49
Smoke and Mirrors, 171, 199
Sobel, Louis, 8
SOFA Productions, 101, 185–87
Solt, Andrew, 101–02, 194
Spencer Hare Publicity Agency, 193
Spoleto Festival, 7, 179
Star, 49
Starr, Ringo, 58–59, 113. *See* also The Beatles
State Ballet of Missouri, 158
Steiger, Rod, 105
Stern, Isaac, xii, 95, 100, 139–40, 157
Sterner, Larry, 158
The Steve Allen Show, 53, 121, 141, 146
Stevens, Risë, 89, 106
Stratas, Teresa, 154
St. Regis Hotel, 126
Streisand, Barbra, 175
Strouse, Charles, 55
Sullivan, Betty. *See* Precht, Betty Sullivan
Sullivan, Daniel, 15
Sullivan, Ed, xi–xii, 1, 3–13, 15–23, 25–31, 33–51, 53–55, 57–59, 62, 65, 67–69, 71–81, 83–87, 89–95, 97, 99–113, 115–20, 122–27, 129–31, 133–36, 142–43, 145–48, 150–53, 160–75, 177, 179–80
Sullivan, Sylvia, 20, 22, 29–30, 33, 34, 37, 58, 75, 125, 161
Sullivan Productions, xiii, 25, 27, 28, 57, 60, 66, 78, 101, 152, 169, 190

Sun Records, 56
The Supremes, 77, 162, 186
Sutherland, Joan, xi, 93, 101–02, 106, 159, 161
Swan Lake, 106
Sylvester, Bob, 8, 48

Takarazuka dancers, 106
Tamarack Lodge, 93
Tebaldi, Renata, 90, 102
Television Hall of Fame, 6
The Temptations, 77, 175, 186
Texaco Star Theater Show, 150
There Shall Be No Night, 104
This American Life, 65
Thompson, Tommy, 61
Three Sopranos, 98
Three Tenors, 98, 180
Tiarks, Mark, 159–160
Time Life, 185–186
Time magazine, xiii, 11–13, 59, 193
Times Square, 78
Tiny Tim, 153
Toast of the Town (column), 8–9, 18–20, 22, 25, 47, 97, 117, 119, 151, 170–71, 173
Toast of the Town, xi, 21, 116, 118, 171, 181. See also *The Ed Sullivan Show*
Toastette dancers, 21
The Today Show, 7, 50
The Tonight Show with Jay Leno, 7, 50, 66, 99
The Tonight Show with Johnny Carson, 66, 69, 101
Topo Gigio, 83–86, 113, 126, 159–60, 186
Tosca, 90, 102, 106
Total Magazine, 57
Tovarich, 152
Trendex, 90
A Tribute to Toscanini, 149
Tri-Cities Opera Company, 156
True Stories, 17
Tucker, Richard, 89–90, 93, 102
Tucker, Sophie, 110, 116
TV Guide, 28, 87, 194

Uggams, Leslie, 77, 162
"Una vocoe poco fa," 102
Underhill, Charles, 117–18
The Untouchables, 151
U.S. Open (golf tournament), 16
U.S. State Department Cultural Exchange Program, 44

Vale, Jerry, 29
Vale, Rita, 29
Van Dyke, Dick, 55
Variety, 18, 49
Velvel, 83
Venus Observed, 104
The Very Best of The Ed Sullivan Show: *Unforgettable Performances, Special Collector's Edition*, 187
The Very Best of The Ed Sullivan Show, *Volume 1: Unforgettable Performances*, 187
The Very Best of The Ed Sullivan Show, *Volume 2: The Greatest Entertainers*, 187
"Vesti il guiba," 102
Victoria Regina, 104
Victor the Bear, xii, 44–46
Villella, Edward, 163
Virginia Opera, 159
"Vissi d'arte," 102
The Voice of Firestone, 98, 122–23, 154, 156
Vorhees, Don, 98

Walker, William, 157
The Wallendas, xii, 106–07
Walt Disney's Wonderful World of Color, 181
Warga, Wayne, 13
Waterloo Bridge, 104
Waters, Ethel, 77, 104
Watts, Charlie, 113
Wayne and Shuster, 110
Weaver, Sylvester "Pat," 150–51, 178
Westchester Country Club, 16

"Where Do We Go from Here?," 103
White House, 71–75
White, Myrna, 81
"Who's Afraid of the Big Bad Wolf?", 104
Will and Grace, 6
William Morris Agency, 55–56, 121
Williams, Hank, 56
Williams, Tennessee, 7
Will Mastin Trio, 79
Wilson, Earl, 8, 48, 193
Wilson, Flip, 77, 167–68
Winchell, Paul, 116
Winchell, Walter, xi, 8–9, 17–18, 20, 25, 47–49, 115, 134, 151, 171, 193
Winters, Shelly, 105

The Wisteria Trees, 104
The Wizard of Oz, 105
Wood, Robert (Bob), 137
World Series (1932), 50–51
World Series (1969), 7
World's Fair, 38
World War II, 20, 116
Wray, John, 118
Wrigley Field, 50
Wyman, Bill, 113

Yankee Stadium, 98
"Young at Heart," 110
Youngman, Henny, 162
"Young People's Concerts," 98

Zelig, 171
Ziegfeld, Florenz, 110, 112

About the Author

Bernie Ilson has been running his own public relations company in New York City since 1963, when his first client was Sullivan Productions, the producers of *The Ed Sullivan Show*. Mr. Ilson's clients have also included Motown Records, Bell Records, the Grammy Awards, the Country Music Awards, Tony Bennett, Benny Goodman, Soupy Sales, Liberty Mutual's Boston Pops television specials, the Missoula Children's Theater, Silver Dollar City, the *Grand Ole Opry*, *Hee Haw*, *The Monkees*, *Candid Camera*, Procter & Gamble, and scores of other artists, television shows, nonprofit agencies, and corporations.

Prior to entering the field of public relations, Mr. Ilson worked as a stand-up comedian and a comedy writer on the NBC Television Comedy Development Program along with another young writer named Woody Allen. Just prior to opening his own agency, Mr. Ilson was a vice president at Rogers and Cowan, the leading public relations firm in the world of entertainment.

Mr. Ilson earned a B.A. from Brooklyn College, an M.A. from Columbia University, and a Ph.D. in culture and communications from New York University in 1998. He has taught public relations at Baruch College in New York City and is listed in the last ten editions of "Who's Who in America" and "Who's Who in the World." Mr. Ilson and his wife, Carol, reside in New York City, and have two sons, David and Jimmy, and four grandchildren. Mr. Ilson is also a well-known watercolor artist and has had three one-man shows in New York City. His work has also been shown at the Brooklyn Museum.